so help me dog

Also by Joe Bennett:
Just Walking the Dogs
(Hazard Press)
Sleeping Dogs and Other Lies
(Hazard Press)
Fun Run and Other Oxymorons
(Simon & Schuster/Scribner UK)

so help me dog

joe bennett

All articles in this book were first
published in the Christchurch *Press*,
the *Evening Post*, the *New Zealand Herald*,
Hawke's Bay Today, the *Otago Daily Times*
or the *New Zealand Listener.*

First published 2000
Reprinted 2002, 2003

ISBN 1-877270-02-4

Published by Hazard Press Ltd
P.O. Box 2151, Christchurch, New Zealand
Front cover photograph by John McCombe

Printed in New Zealand

Contents

Foreword

I am tempted to write about writing, but I have little to add to what I've said in previous books and, besides, I am mindful of mechanics. Mechanics who have mended my car always want to tell me what they've done to the carburettor. I just want the car to go.

I don't know if mechanics spend a lot of time thinking about engines. I spend a lot of time thinking about writing but it doesn't do any good. The only way to write is to write. Sometimes words come easily but often they don't. For me writing means rewriting. Technique is a cloak to hide the strain.

I write by ear. When I think I've finished a piece I need to read it aloud to find that I haven't. Reading to the dogs is unsatisfactory, so I would like to thank John and Averil and John and John and Kerry and Robyn and Bridget and Jim and Christine and Sarah and other poor sods for bearing with me when I ring to read them stuff. They are kind and patient people.

J.B, Lyttelton, 2000

She smuggled a tortoise

'World,' wrote Louis MacNeice, 'is crazier and more of it than we think.' I have known these words for years and have indeed bored class after class of children with them. The children have yawned, I suspect, because to them the idea is obvious. But in middle age I find I lose sight of the truth of MacNeice's words. The world seems weary, stale, flat and unprofitable. But then something happens to remind me that it is sweetly crazy. This week, for example, I met a tortoise-smuggler.

The woman has smuggled only one tortoise, but that is one tortoise more than I have smuggled or am likely to smuggle.

Smuggler and tortoise met in Corfu, an island where the tortoise is apparently indigenous. This particular specimen, a small one, appeared by her bed one morning in the villa which she was renting. She took momentary fright, but the tortoise made no threatening move so she scooped it with a tray and bore it to the garden where she laid it gently down and watched it unfurl its neck and legs, nibble a snatch of something green for sustenance then head once more for the house. She raced it back and shut the door.

That evening the tortoise was at the step, whining silently to be let in. She left the door open. In the morning the tortoise was beside her bed. She let it stay, feeding it scraps of vegetable matter and sometimes a little pasta. It seemed contented and stayed for the remainder of her holiday. Once or twice she trod on it, but it did not take offence. She grew fond of it, she said.

I did not know that tortoises could show enough character to arouse affection. But this one had been, if nothing else, persistent and she said she liked its undemanding manner and also the curious way it drank.

At the end of the holiday she was loath to leave the tortoise. She did not flatter herself that the tortoise had attached itself specifically to her, but neither did she trust the next occupants of the villa to treat it with due kindness. She resolved to take it home to London with her.

She made enquiries of the authorities which deal with such things, and learned that it was illegal to import tortoises to Great Britain without a permit. Rabies was the problem. Corfu has rabies and Great Britain doesn't. Now the woman in question is a responsible citizen. She insures her car and rarely drops litter and does not bury garden rubbish in her council bin bags. But when she weighed the issue she resolved that Great Britain had little to fear from a single tiny tortoise, even if it were later to foam at the mouth and go on rabid rampage.

So when she left she sat the tortoise in the bottom of her carry-on luggage along with an apple core and a carrot to keep it amused on the journey. As she passed through customs at Heathrow she felt the gaze of a dull-booted officer. She caught his eye, looked too swiftly away and was summoned. The officer rummaged unsmilingly through her suitcase, turning over her underwear and nightdresses and shaking a doll in native costume which she had bought for a niece. Then he indicated her shoulder bag. With tremulous fingers she emptied the contents onto his table, feeling no doubt as the frightfully rich American must have felt when the sniffer dog barked at his bag, although he, of course, was rightly let off on the grounds that if he had come to watch the America's Cup yachting then he needed every drug he could get.

The customs officer fingered her cosmetics, her tube of disposable contact lenses and then the tiny tortoise. It had, understandably, retracted its wrinkled head and feet. She said it was a brooch. The customs officer impounded the carrot and the apple core and let her go.

When she reached home she found the tortoise had eaten her lipstick and it was dead.

It is a little story and a sad one, but it filled me and thrilled me, in MacNeice's words, with 'the drunkenness of things being various'.

A prayer to Mrs Shaughnessy

O Mrs Shaughnessy, I am gathered here together in the presence of dogs and in the sure and certain hope that kindness is a boomerang. O Mrs Shaughnessy, I beseech thee, hear my prayer. Amen.

The lesson is taken from the Book of Incompetent Men, beginning to read at 7 o'clock last Wednesday.

And it came to pass that a certain horny-handed scribe laid down his word processor and journeyed into Christchurch to see a play by a man called Stoppard, and the play did crackle so with wit and learning that the scribe understood none of it. But he said not so, for fear that others in the assembly should set upon him and beat him and leave him for a dunce.

From theatre to carpark crept the scribe. The night was still and frozen and particulates did hang upon the air, and the scribe discovered his windscreen shrouded so in mystery that he would have to drive home hunched over the steering wheel and seeing through a glass darkly. But more and worse befell the scribe for he perceived with horror that his car had been set upon by misfortune which had wounded a rear tyre and stripped it of air and left it for dead.

Now this scribe was a foolish man who had let his membership of the Automobile Association lapse, so he drew from the rear of the car after long struggling the thing they did call in those parts a jack, and he knelt on the frozen carpark like a sorry congregation of one and he did guess where the jack should sit beneath the car and with numb fingers he fitted the winding piece and he wound. And as he wound, lo, he scraped his horny knuckles on the ground and much was the tearing of flesh and the dripping of blood and the wailing of teeth and the gnashing of the larynx and the emission of oaths. And the scribe did bind his wounds with a handkerchief and he sat down upon the frozen land and he wept. And I say unto you the particulates of the air did seem to frown upon him.

But a certain pair of Samaritans came where he was and when they saw him they had compassion on him and they did burst out laughing. 'Ho ho, mate,' they did cry, 'you got a flattie. We'll soon fix that.'

The scribe looked up and he forgot the aching of his wounds, and he forgot the wailing of his teeth, and to his feet he rose, and crying 'no' and 'no' again he seized once more the winding piece and mightily he wound as though the vengeance of the Lord were upon him and nipping at his buttocks. And 'She'll be right,' he cried, and 'Thanks, but I'll be fine. A scribe I may be, but a horny-handed one and I can change a tyre.'

The Samaritans they looked from each to each and then again they laughed. 'Ha ha,' they said. The scribe replied 'Ha ha', for though he did not know what they were laughing at, he thought it best to seem as if he did.

'O horny-handed scribe,' said one Samaritan, 'you know not what you do. You don't wind up the jack until you've loosened all the nuts. Here pass the thing to me.' And speaking thus the one Samaritan did seize the jack, the other fetched the brace and as a pair they set about the job. The scribe stood useless in the frozen air and frantically he looked about lest someone he might know should pass that way, for though the scribe delighted in the changing of the wheel, he did not wish the world to know that both the good Samaritans were – the congregation will now gasp – women.

Yea, verily, these splendid souls who thus took pity on the scribe were Liz and Jill. They fetched a cloth to lay upon the ground, a cloth which Liz referred to as her wedding dress, and as Liz loosened all the nuts with fearsome arm, and Jill, as was appropriate, fixed the jack, the gladsome twosome told a string of jokes that set the helpless hapless scribe a-roaring in the frosted air.

Jill told him that this wasn't what she'd call a genuine flat tyre, it being only flat at the bottom, but still with skill that put the scribe to shame she hauled the old tyre off and Liz attached the spare and all was well.

It grieved the scribe that he could offer nothing for their pains but cigarettes. But these they took with smiles and, blowing clouds of smoke to dance with the particulates of the night, they wandered off to seek out others to do good unto.

And this, O Mrs Shaughnessy, is where I pray to thee. For Liz, the lass in shining armour, is a teacher, and thou, O Mrs Shaughnessy, art her boss. And thy employee Liz is desperate for an extra day of holiday for reasons she'll explain. And because, Mrs Shaughnessy, I believe that kindness is a boomerang which returns to bless the inventor, I am confident that thou wilt grant her request and that this scribe will be forever in thy debt.

Ahoy

When I was a kid there were lots of words I couldn't spell, but only two I knew I couldn't spell. I can spell them now, of course, but I still remember the confusion they caused me. One was Egypt and the other was yot.

The dictionary I intend to write defines a yot as 'a stationary possession disguised as a mode of transport, occupied by a fool, and bounded on one side by water and on the other by a berth priced at the GDP of Belgium'. The same dictionary defines Egypt as a hot place I haven't visited.

Much have I travelled in the realms of gold, and, I would add, many goodly states and kingdoms seen, but I have never been tempted by Egypt. Of Egypt I know only the pyramids and I don't understand them. I believe none of the nonsense about their being used for astronomical calculation, and as domestic architecture they're disastrous. I'd rather die than live in one.

Cleopatra was a famous Egyptian. President Nasser was the other one. By a curious coincidence, Cleopatra happened to be the world's first yotsperson. Shakespeare described her yot as a barge, but he was in love with Tom Stoppard at the time and preoccupied with a screenplay. A yot it was, and like a burnished throne for that matter, with a couple of pyramids in the fo'c'sle (pronounced forecastle) as a sort of sextant. President Nasser was not a yotsperson, but the Americans still named their space agency after him in the hope of flattering him into telling them the astronomical secrets of the Pyramids.

So, as you can see, I'm up to speed with yots and yotting, the history, practice and navigation thereof, so when a close neighbour and distant friend of mine who has often expressed an urge to keelhaul my dogs, invited me out for a quick schmozzle round Lyttelton Harbour on his spanking new 36-footer it was the work of a moment for me to hide under the house.

But he's not the sort of fellow to let seaweed grow under his feet, and before you could say hoist the mains'l I found myself down at what we old sea dogs call the edge of the water, dressed for the voyage in an oilskin and a rather fetching blue funk. The old salt invited me aboard by pushing me off the jetty. He then suggested I earn my keep by hauling on the painter and weighing the anchor. The painter seemed to have withdrawn to the pub but I resisted the urge to join him by skilfully inserting the tail of my oilskin into the captain's hands while pretending to climb ashore.

Pausing only to toss my will to a passing cormorant, I signalled to the skipper that all was shipshape under the mizzen and we cast off. Suddenly we were at sea, with only a skin of fibreglass between me and the ravening dolphins, and as the deck pitched beneath my feet I felt that exhilaration that makes us yotties yot.

Driven to express my exhilaration I headed for the heads (pronounced poopdeck), where I found my sea-legs, screwed them on and was back on deck in a trice (pronounced two and a half hours). Aloft once more and feeling chipper as a corpse, I trimmed the gymbals, spliced the spinnaker, braced the bowsprit and made a suggestion. 'Let me off,' I suggested in the measured tone of a spoilt three-year-old.

From the discomfort of his air-conditioned wheelhouse the old sea dog was all sympathy. 'Prepare to tack, me hearty,' he bellowed into the teeth of the gale which swallowed his words at a gulp and grinned for more, 'going about.'

There is a merry little thing on board all yots called the boom. It's a sort of two-ton scythe. The entertaining purpose of a boom is to catch us tars on the back of the skull, but I am too tarry a tar to fall for the boom-in-the-back-of-the-head trick. As we yawled our gunwales to windward I sensed the boom's approach and turned just in time to catch it neatly on the right temple.

After briefly pondering the range of options available to me, I chose to lose consciousness. It is an old truth of the sea that the pleasures of yotting increase in direct proportion to the degree of coma. When I came to, we were dibbling back into the marina. Masking my disappointment with a chorus of 'yessirree' and a celebratory jig round a mainsheet (pronounced rope), I leapt ashore.

'Leapt' is precisely the right verb. 'Ashore' is about half a metre away from being the right adverb.

'Ho ho,' sympathised the old sea dog. I bade him a cheerful farewell with the gesture known to yotties as Cleopatra's Needle and went home (pronounced home).

Aubergine therapy

Until recently I knew little about modern medicine. I was a robust child and I met my doctor only three times. The first was when he attended my birth but I ignored him. I was too intent, at the time, on launching my lifelong career in bawling for attention.

I didn't meet my doctor properly until I was eight. That was when I caught my foreskin in the zip of my trousers. I found it impossible to tell my mother what had happened, so I told my brother. He found it impossible not to tell my mother and everyone else in the neighbourhood. Soon afterwards the doctor arrived in my bedroom clutching a large pair of boltcutters. As it turned out, the boltcutters were not required and the doctor fixed the problem with decisive swiftness once my mother had peeled me from the ceiling.

The only other time I met the doctor I brought him an ankle like an aubergine. I had twisted it playing soccer and I believed it broken. The doctor twisted it some more in a manner which I found most amusing and then told me an x-ray was unnecessary, that time would work its recuperative wonder and that I would be playing soccer again in three weeks. I was.

Earlier this year I twisted my other ankle. I sustained the injury on the squash court rather than the soccer pitch, but the acute pain and the decorative effect were identical. And after a session in the surgery which reminded me of all the fun of thirty years before, the doctor pronounced that the ankle required a course of physiotherapy.

Now I may have known little about conventional medicine but I knew even less about physiotherapy. I knew that, like consultancy, it was a boom industry of the nineties, but otherwise I bracketed it vaguely with all the other therapies – psycho, aroma, retail and so on. My only connection with these, and a tenuous one at best, was that I call the starter cord on my lawnmower 'the chiropractor' because it is unlikely to do any good to my back.

If pressed I would have said that physiotherapy involved vigorous wrenching and bending and my first sight of Mr Physio confirmed that idea. He wore I'm-healthy shorts and bore that scrawny, muscular look of the dedicated mountain-biker which is so often mistaken for sanity. But he neither wrenched nor bent me. He used gadgets.

First he smeared me with erotic gel, then he rubbed my ankle with a blunt instrument. It seemed to promise much but I felt nothing. Mr Physio explained that this was ultrasound, a sort of inaudible Lite FM. Apparently it soothes troubled muscles by singing to them at a pitch that is popular with bats.

Having soothed the leg he then tortured it. Acupuncture works on the principle that a needle stuck into one place will affect a different place. So, I believe, does voodoo.

'You may feel a slight tingling,' said the physiotherapist. I didn't feel a slight tingling. I felt a needle going into my knee. Bleeding was minimal, however, and I enjoyed the process in much the same way as an athletics official enjoys visiting A & E wearing a javelin.

The third stage of my treatment featured a close relative of the machine which they used to apply to the heads of schizophrenics. The physio taped electrodes to my ankle and zapped me. And having instructed me to turn the dial to any level that I found comfortable, he left to zap someone else.

The level that I found comfortable was zero. But the man on the next bed was undergoing the same treatment and the urge to compete beats strongly in the male chest. When the physio returned, both of us were humming like tuning forks. I was 3 volts away from the recommended dose for murderers in Florida.

I returned in the days that followed for two more sessions of physio. Gradually the swelling subsided, the aubergine faded, the muscles recovered and I returned to the squash court. And, most remarkable of all, it took precisely three weeks.

Bedside lovers

I cannot imagine not reading. Some books, of course, are like lovers; you go to bed with them once and fall asleep immediately. My bedside table is piled with such books, which I have started but will never finish. They lie face-down in heaps, frozen open at an early page, like a stack of dead moths. Sometimes a stack topples and the books lie for months on the floor, their spines permanently deformed.

But other books become house guests. They take up residence in rooms of the mind and never leave. If I sit quietly I can hear the footfalls of several authors in the grey and looping corridors of my head. Albert Camus pads around up there in his suit, smoking Algerian cigarettes and never smiling. On his way to the bathroom he passes a fat, smug Evelyn Waugh and doesn't even nod to him. None of the authors, indeed, pay any attention to each other. But each can sing and each has sung to me.

The books which have lodged in my skull I read mostly between the ages of sixteen and twenty-two. I have heard people say that character is formed by the age of seven. They may say true, but thought is formed later, I think, and so are some forms of sentiment. These writers soldered the wiring of parts of my mind, such that there are times when I feel with their fingers, think with their words, tap my toes to their rhythms.

I do not always recognise the debt, but sometimes when I say a phrase or think a thought I hear a grumble from a distant room, and I realise that the phrase or thought is borrowed from one of my house guests. So I go to my shelves and pull down the book and sink back into its world. I soon forget to seek the line I had echoed and am absorbed by the hypnosis of the language. It is like pushing open the door of the pub and seeing an old and dear friend at the bar with an empty stool beside him and a full glass.

So it was recently. Something took me back to Laurie Lee, and I spent the day reading *As I Walked Out One Midsummer Morning* for perhaps the fifteenth time.

As always I found something new: 'Eating bread and sausage, my back to the church wall, I was aware only of this point in time, the arrested moment of casual detail, the unsorted rubbish of now. I felt the heat of the sun dampened by draughts of ice blowing from fish-boxes stacked nearby. I remember a yawning cat – a pin-cushion of teeth and whiskers – sitting on a palm-leaf in the gutter. A man said 'Good morning' and passed out of my life, stepping on a petal as though extinguishing a match.'

That scene lasted a few seconds. But sixty-five years later I can see the man and his boot and the petal more clearly than I can see anything in this dusty room I am writing in. I can see it indeed more clearly than if I were shown film of it.

But the phrase that matters is 'the unsorted rubbish of now'. We live in a dump of detail, a welter of tiny nothings, of heels descending on petals and of cats yawning. They make no sense. They are unsorted rubbish. It takes a Laurie Lee to sort the rubbish, to transmute it into permanence, to make a false, seductive coherence out of what does not cohere.

A while ago I had my ears syringed. As happens every year, they had become plugged with wax. My hearing had dulled. I had adjusted to the thin trickle of sound that squeezed through. When I emerged from the surgery, sound assaulted me. Rain beat a tattoo on an awning. Car tyres hissed like cats. I caught bites of conversation from across the street. Through the open window of a pub I heard a woman talking about the death of a horse.

Reading can do something similar. It can syringe the ears, ream the nostrils, scrub the fingertips, scour the tongue and peel the eyes. I cannot imagine not reading.

Gone goat

Don't look over your shoulder. It brings only grief. For behind us lies the land of might-have-been, irrecoverable, receding into the distance as the steamboat of time carries us out into the ocean of nonentity. The coastline of might-have-been becomes a smudge on the horizon then fades for ever into the limitless nowhere of the sea of middle-class middle age. It is profoundly sad.

Such potential we had when we were young. Where did it go? For sure it has gone, faded liked smoke, melded indistinguishably into the bland air, and all our dreams gone with it.

When I look back I see a seven-year-old at a party. That boy was me and back then I knew stuff. I knew that life was a game of sheep and goats and I wanted to be on the side of whichever animal it was that won. On balance I fancied the goats. I still do. They have better horns, better digestive systems and they eat washing.

The party was thrown by a fat boy to indulge his gluttony, and we all duly trooped along to glut with him and to play pass the parcel. I could glut with the best of them but I was better still at pass the parcel. I cheated. I seized the parcel from girls before my turn. I hung onto it longer than I should. I tore at its wrappings with my teeth. There was a prize inside that parcel and I meant it to be mine. I was raw goat.

I won, of course. The prize came in a little box. I opened the box and found it empty. The prize was the box. But though the box had nothing inside it, I did. I had greed. I was goat. The goat burst into tears.

I hunted down the fat boy's fat mother and I wailed. She said the box was a nice box and that was that. She went away. I followed her. I followed her like a goat after washing. I wanted a better prize. Whenever the fat mother turned she tripped over a seven-year-old in tears and Marks and Spencer sandals. With my undissuadable mix of persistence and emotional manipulation I wore her down. She gave me a different prize. I have forgotten what it was.

But I haven't forgotten the attitude. If only I had retained such tenacity. But it has gone, all gone. Today, crippled by fear, and an outmoded sense of courtesy and the needs of others and the wish to avoid a scene, I take what I am given. Today I would be more likely to say, 'Oh no, don't bother. Actually I rather like the empty box. It is, if you like, a sort of metaphor for the hollowness of mere acquisition, a cross between a caveat emptor and a memento mori for the consumer society, don't you think? Indeed it is by far the best prize I have ever won. I am thrilled by my empty box. Please don't trouble yourself in the least about finding a substitute prize. I could hardly be closer to ecstasy. I say, what wonderful wallpaper. Did you stencil it yourself?'

The years have taught me to lie. Back then I was all innocent honesty. Give, I said, and meant it, and stuck with it, barren of rhetoric, devoid of politesse. I was goat, all emphatic, imperative greed, and wholly admirable. And it worked. Contrary to all the pious nonsense of grandma and other defeated adults, he who asks does get, and he goes on getting and getting until he dies with a houseful of pass-the-parcel prizes in Parnell.

What could I not have done? With that rapacity and single-minded devotion to self I could have been a chisel-faced banker. I could have cut deals and screwed the opposition, and trodden on fingers and found venture capital and been knighted for services to myself. I could have animated advertisements for breakfast cereals. I could have talked glibly of quality-driven, client-focused synergy and pocketed the dosh. I could have gone drinking with Vince Lombardi and when he said 'Winning isn't everything – it's the only thing', I could have slapped him on the back and ordered another highball. I could have reaped the harvest of greed and manipulation and all the other virtues that society rewards while it pretends to despise them. I could have inherited the earth. Oh it would have been wonderful. But instead I got meek.

Where did I go wrong? Where is my goat of yesteryear? Gone, long gone. Too late, old boy, the saddest words in the English language.

Cheers for booze

Now is the season when family and friends come together in a spirit of festivity and get drunk. And what fun they have. Take a mob of malcontent dyspeptic uncles, frowzy aunts and mumbling grannies, drop a crate of Chateau Fizzy in their midst and watch the graph of pleasure soar.

The world abounds in lies. The three most famous are 'the cheque's in the mail', 'I love you' and another I can never remember. I can think of a plethora of candidates for that third spot – 'New Zealand First' comes to mind, or 'statistical proof', or any sentence containing the word 'honestly' – but the strongest and commonest of all the lies that encrust our mendacious little lives is that booze is a depressant. No matter how the medicos define depressant, I know depression and it does not come in bottles.

The same people as tell you this lie will tell you that tea is a stimulant. Have they never sat around a pot of tea and a plate of fancy cakes discussing knitting patterns with a bunch of women in tweed? No they haven't, and nor have I and I don't intend to. Any event that serves tea is funereal. If you want me I'll be in the pub.

Every human society has found a way of making booze. Only a few have tried to undo that knowledge. All have been fools and wrong. During Prohibition, for example, more drink tipped down American throats than ever tipped before or since. Those few countries where drink is illegal are the countries where hands are chopped off, feuds incessant and religion fanatical. And all the chiefs and bosses, sheikhs and sahibs knock it back a-plenty on the sly.

But, astonishingly, there's a deep and ugly streak of wowserism here in young New Zealand. No doubt it stems from fascinating historical causes which I want to know nothing about. It leaps to its feet when any liberal move is mooted. Women with clenched mouths, arched eyebrows and unthinkable frocks bemoan the moral decline. Bull-necked men with fat smug ties quiver at the jowls at the lowering of the drinking age, the dissolution of the church and the collapse of family values.

Most recently the legal drinking age came down from twenty to eighteen and oh the fuss of wowserdom about it all. And do the youthful topers now run rampage through the night? And are our streets awash with howling teenage drunks? Of course they are. And so they were last year, and so the year before. But no, you're right, they weren't awash with teenage drunks in 1956 because the teenage drunks were hiding in the bush with woollen underwear and a stolen flagon of applejack. But that, of course, was kids being kids and having harmless fun.

And so it was. And so it is.

The wowsers call booze alcohol. They lie. If booze is alcohol then steak is nutrients and you and I are water. Booze is brandy, gin and wine; it's beer and rum and Amaretto, all rich and luscious words of ancient origin and faultless pedigree.

But the killjoys and the puritans will take me by the hand and lead me to the women's refuge and they will show me the suffering caused by drunks. And then they'll lead me to the morgue and show me drunken drivers smashed to bits and sober passengers with injuries that horrify.

Yes, yes, but then I will take them by the hand and lead them to the Lava Bar where men and women who have nothing in common but the freedom to be there, the money to spend there and too much to worry about are laughing. I will show them happy people. Or to the pub in Wellington we'll go and I will show them bureaucrats on Friday night whose ties have come undone and who no longer speak of target outcomes but are using nouns and verbs of simple honesty and whose jaws are sore from laughter. For every ounce of suffering I'll show a ton of lubricated joy.

Booze isn't respectable, of course. Anything that fosters honesty or pleasure is sure to be condemned in a society founded on repression. Booze lifts repression, dissolves inhibition and any psychologist will tell you over a glass of the best and finest what dreadful damage we do to ourselves with inhibitions. Drink is cheap psychotherapy. Drink opens the jailhouse door. It doesn't delude, it just shortens the gap between thought and action. Drunks are more likely to say what they think and do what they want. And that is a very good thing. And despite the crashed cars and the damaged people and the stumblers with meths, as a general rule the gods look after drunks. Or at least they've looked after me. I can point at a wall in France which should have killed me. I can point at a donkey in the River Ebro and two cathedral roofs. I can point at memories that make me gurgle with delight. And so can thousands upon thousands.

Of course apologists for booze have tried to dress the stuff in Sunday best. They speak of responsible drinking as if the phrase were not by definition, praise the Lord, an oxymoron. And those who fangle metaphors for wine, who speak of crisp herbaceous noses, toasty finishes and hints of passionfruit are merely coining fancy words for fun. For yes, all wines taste different but not once you have got beyond the second sip. And now they've tried to do the same for beer. I know a newspaper that runs a column on beer. Oh spare us. Old Kingsley Amis, dead as mutton now, expressed it best, when he said all advertisements for beer could be reduced to one generic slogan: 'Drink Blank beer. It makes you pissed.'

Booze is a vast industry and an essential one. To ease our consciences we tax the stuff ferociously but still we pour it down. What staggers me is not how much damage booze wreaks, but how little, and in exchange it grants such easing of the mind, so much untrammelled laughter.

Dost thou think, because thou art virtuous, there shall be no more cakes and ale? Go sir, rub your chain with crumbs.

Happy New Year.

Rite rite

They must exist the whole year round, I suppose, but I hear of them only occasionally. One of those occasions was last week when they popped their heads above the parapets once more and squeaked their dangerous nonsense.

They are the Simplified Spelling Society – or, presumably, the Simplifide Speling Sosiyutee. The Simplies have been around for a long time and have never got very far, but I don't see that as any reason to stop me sticking the boot into their ideas.

I have never met a Simplie but I imagine them to be bearded people in sweaters the colour of vinegar. No doubt they're not. No doubt they're all clean-shaven and decorated in nice bright acrylic sweaters from Deka, and no doubt they breed lovely children and give generously to charity, but my image of them is born of my distaste for their ideas. They would like to fiddle with the English language. I would like to cut their fiddling fingers off.

Although the English language has provided me with a living of sorts for a couple of decades, I have yet only the scantiest knowledge of its complexities. English is like a coral reef. It has grown over the centuries by a process of slow accretion and slower erosion. It has fed on everything that has floated past it and absorbed what it has found useful. Though the fat dictionaries may suggest the language is a fixed and lumpish thing, it is alive and in constant change.

It is also resilient. It allows all manner of politicians, sports commentators and guidance counsellors to torture it, and yet it retains a sinuous strength that rebounds undamaged from all assaults.

Because the roots of English lie partly in Anglo-Saxon and partly in Latin and partly in French, and because English has accommodated offerings from a host of other tongues, and because it has been put to use in a mass of different climates and circumstances, and because it has always welcomed change,

English has become a difficult language to spell. Through does not rhyme with though, nor with cough or bough or enough or thorough. I find that delightful. The Simplies don't. If they had their way these words would become something like thru, tho, coff, bow, enuf and thura.

And no doubt the Simplies would argue that they would thus make the language easier to read and write. Their argument would certainly find favour with such august institutions as the Ministry of Education and the New Zealand Qualifications Authority who have applied the same principle to exams: if children can't pass them then the obvious solution is to make the exams easier.

The educational mandarins are proved wrong every day and the Simplies are similarly wrong. Even if spelling were utterly logical and consistent, just as many children would spell badly. Maths, for example, is logical and consistent yet plenty of children fail to grasp it.

I have taught several thousand children. Some could spell and some couldn't and most lay in between. By and large those who could spell were readers and those who couldn't weren't. I also taught plenty of children who had been told they were dyslexic and not a few who actually were. But I found that, with hard work, even the most severe dyslexics could gain some mastery over their problems. They could even learn to spell dyslexia. They certainly had a harder road to ride than people like me who find it easy to spell almost everything except inoculate and gauge, but I do not believe that the language should be altered to suit people who find spelling hard. It would be like taking the high jump out of the Olympics because some people have short legs.

Most words carry their history with them. Their roots can be found in the spelling. Change the spelling and those roots would be harder to trace. Though language moves on and meanings alter, and etymology rarely grants us the present meaning of a word, nevertheless when the winds of stupidity blow roots can act as an anchor.

But not only would the simplification of spelling distance the language from its roots, more importantly still it would sever the people of tomorrow from the wisdom of yesterday. A reasonably educated speaker of English can read Chaucer in the original. Mess about with the spelling and Chaucer would become as impenetrable as Sanskrit. So would Shakespeare, Dickens, Bacon, Eggers and *Goodbye Mr Chips*.

Lose your past and you lose everything. All the thinking has to be done over again. The language brings with it the gains and the wisdom of yesterday.

The first act of the totalitarian leaders of 1984 was to modernise the language and thus to cripple independent thought and the gains of history. All unwitting, the Simplies wish to commit a similar Orwellian atrocity on our tongue. No doubt they mean well but they would encourage the descent of the Dark Ages. Theirs is an innocent arrogance.

Eating with experts

Today I woke to hear an expert – and I am terribly fond of experts – recounting on the radio the joys of the Mediterranean diet. I missed the first part of the interview so I did not hear which Mediterranean diet he was extolling. I wondered if perhaps he meant the Greek diet of octopus and goat cheese or the Libyan diet of dictatorship and poverty, or perhaps the Palestinian diet of rubber bullets. But I gathered, I think, that he meant a trendy Italian diet of olives, pasta, salads, Vespas, bambini, linguini and Catholicism. This diet, said the man, would lengthen our lives.

Our expert told us with gloom in his voice that the New Zealand diet is slow suicide. It gives us cancer, stills our fluttering hearts. All that fat, he said, it kills us.

Now I do not know if this expert was the same expert who told me last year that the Japanese diet of fish, rice and lightly braised kimonos was the one that would lengthen my life. He certainly had the same tone in his voice, that mix of zeal and lamentation. Or was he perhaps last week's expert who told me that chocolate would kill me? Or there again he may have been this week's expert who told me that chocolate was good for me, that indeed it would enhance both my shelf-life and my sex-life. Since I heard that news, of course, I've been shovelling down the Cadbury's and I can already tell you he's at least 50 per cent wrong. When I know about the other 50 per cent I'll let you know.

So perhaps he was the expert who wrote the magazine questionaire which I dutifully completed in the dentist's waiting room only to find that I was an alcoholic, doomed to grow a liver like a cauliflower and to pop my cork within months. Or perhaps he was the expert who told me, to my great relief, that if I wanted to be as sprightly as a rat, the first thing I should do each morning was to gargle a couple of glasses of cabernet sauvignon.

There again he could have been closely related to the scientific expert who brought free radicals to my attention, those dramatic little independent entities espousing obscure political causes, which can, I believe, either kill me or render me immortal – I forget which but it is always the one or the other.

Or was he the man who goes around putting ticks on tins, or the one who spends his life usefully measuring the fat content of the pastry in meat pies? Or the woman who made millions from a book about cleaning your liver? Was he even the man who looked like a stringbean, who invented jogging and who keeled over at the age of fifty-five in mid-jog? Or perhaps he was the man who tells me that I have to drink 8 litres of water a day, or even the splendid chap who tells me that smoking fends off Alzheimer's, presumably by killing me before I can go doolally.

Well, he is all of these people and none of them. He is every dietary expert under the merry sun. He is also a busybody and a Jeremiah. I do not need him and nor, for a host of reasons, do you.

For a start, he is often giving us information that will be contradicted next week. As a child I remember being told, for example, that potatoes would make me fat.

But even if his propaganda were proveable fact, he would still only be telling me more or less what my body knows. If I drink too much I get a hangover. It is the body telling me to rein in the horses of licentiousness. I can choose, of course, to let the horses gallop, but the warning is there and the responsibility mine. Similarly, if I eat two scoops of chips and a shoal of deep-fried fish, and round it off with a box of Mars bars, I feel sick. Or if I eat nothing but hamburgers I grow constipated and weary. I may be fool enough to ignore those warnings, but that is my affair.

People have worried about dying since the first clock ticked, and a fat lot of good it has done them. Indeed it has done them harm. I am confident that the surest way to shorten one's life is to worry about how long it is going to be.

And if Italians live longer than New Zealanders – and I don't for one minute believe that they do – they do so because they snooze in the sun, dandle bambini, shovel linguini, take it easy, try to be happy and, most importantly of all, they worry as little as possible and they laugh as much as possible, especially at experts.

I believe in pigs

A pig's orgasm lasts for half an hour.

I learned this splendid nugget a couple of weeks ago and it has since become a fixture in my conversational repertoire. It sparks a lively response at any social event but is best reserved for formal dinner parties. It goes down well with loin of pork.

I learned about the pig from Pat, a music teacher who has never to my knowledge or suspicion, been in a position to verify the truth of his assertion. But that doesn't stop me believing it. The nub of the matter is not that I think it is true, but that I want it to be true.

There is probably a word for this tendency of mine, but I suspect it is a Greek word and I'm afraid all Greek is Greek to me. The word I'm looking for isn't stupidity and it isn't credulousness. I want a word to describe something altogether more wilful which has been the mainstay of my intellectual life. I want a word to describe the tendency of human beings to prefer the excitingly improbable idea to the dull and more probable one.

Why is it, for example, that for thirty years or so I have believed that glass is a liquid? It looks and feels like a solid, it sounds like a solid when I tap it, when I tap it too hard it slices my flesh and yet I have told innumerable people that it is a liquid and for evidence I have pointed out that ancient windows are thicker at the bottom than at the top because, over the course of the centuries, the glass has slowly dripped. Obviously, I have never examined ancient windows to see if it is so, but someone whom I can no longer remember once told me it was so and it sounded exciting to me and so I decided it was so.

And while I am at it, why should I and so many other people have believed that powdered glass in coffee is a recognised method of murder? Powdered glass in coffee would settle as sludge at the bottom of the cup and the victim would have to spoon the murder weapon down his throat himself. And even if he did so the glass would pass harmlessly though his gut. Nevertheless for years I have believed the irrational exciting opposite of the truth.

Just as when people come across flattened wheat they presume not that wind has laid it low or that people or animals have trodden it down but that aliens have travelled hundreds of light years across the galaxy in order to crush a fraction of a cereal crop before going home. And how we all would like it to be true.

And why, when a friend is late for a meeting, do I always imagine that something disastrous has happened, that a car crash has left him mangled in a ditch? And if I am alone in a house at night why, when I hear a noise, do I assume that it is not a possum on the roof or a creak in the weatherboards but rather an intruder with a baseball bat and malice, or a ghost with the face of a skull, so that I withdraw whimpering beneath the blankets?

And why, when probability theory tells the plainest story of folly, do a million people troop to the Lotto shop every Saturday to hand over the money that they love in the strange conviction that they have been singled out?

And why do people who know that we live in a galaxy of cooling lumps of matter circling other cooling lumps of matter cling to the belief, the hope, that destiny is written in the heavens, that the orbit of the planets somehow impinges on the fate of each of us?

And why, when Elvis is dead, for which relief much thanks, should he reappear so frequently in the supermarkets of Tennessee?

Why should these and a thousand other superstitions, myths and fallacies so grasp our minds? For sure the wish is father to the thought but why should the wish exist? Why should we want the world to be more than it is, to offer greater delights, stranger truths, greater mysteries? Could it be that the miraculous truth of life is essentially a mundane miracle and we cannot accept that dust returns to dust, that the great random concatenation of chance and carbon and other stuff is ultimately barren, explicable and purposeless? Is it that our consciousness, that gift which is both boon and burden, cannot be satisfied by brutal fact, cannot accommodate our own mortality, cannot accept that what is, is and there's an end to it?

I'm afraid I do not know. The only thing I know for sure is why pigs appear always to be grinning.

In the bad lands

It rose in front of us, sheer, gaunt and majestic. I gasped. Pete gulped. Side by side we stood to gasp and gulp in wonder. Much had we travelled in the realms of cliché but never had we seen so steep a learning curve.

In comparison with this awesome steepness, every other peak that Pete and I had climbed seemed little more than a level playing field.

We knew immediately that we had no choice. Before us stood the ultimate challenge, our new mission statement. We would tackle this learning curve head on. We would put our noses to the grindstone till they bled. Nothing would stand in the way of our ascent.

'Enjoy,' said Pete with a wry grim smile.

'Enjoy what?' I asked, but he was already away.

Up we plodded, step after laborious step, pausing occasionally to look around us. We knew what we were looking for. We sought a window of opportunity, just a small one that would grant a view of the knowledge economy from the top of the learning curve. But windows of opportunity are few and far between and the going was tough. Obstacles abounded. We waded through income streams and held each other back from cunningly concealed poverty traps.

After twenty-four hours we were on the point of calling it a day when Pete clasped my shoulder.

'Look,' he said.

I looked. On the slope ahead of us, miraculously it seemed, stood a small city square, immaculate with cafés and bars and colonnades. We sank gratefully down at a café table, ordered refreshments from the waitperson and applied ourselves to the problems that faced us. But hard though we thought, no ideas came. Then silently Pete rose and went to stand beyond the furthest building, his chin cupped in his hand. Almost immediately he yelped with delight.

I ran to join him.

'I've got it,' he exclaimed.

'Ah,' I said as the truth dawned on me, 'of course, thinking outside the square. Why didn't I think of that?'

'Never mind that,' said Pete. 'Look!'

I looked and beheld a sight I shall never forget as long as I remember it. There stood the window that we sought and oh what light through yonder window broke. It was the light of opportunity. Without another word Pete and I ran to it, fumbled frantically with the catch, threw open the window and beheld spread out before us... but the story is almost too sad to tell. Our hopes were dashed. They lay in tatters round our ankles. There seemed no point in hauling them back up.

For where we had expected to see the verdant fields of a knowledge economy, or at least the pleasant pastures of a win-win situation, we beheld nothing more and nothing less than the smoking rubble of a worst-case scenario. It was almost too much to bear.

I looked at Pete. Pete looked at me. It would not be stretching a point to say we looked at each other. Despair was etched on our faces. Horror was tattooed on our chests. Hopelessness was scribbled on our thighs. There was nothing for it. We had only one card left to play and we played it.

Pete reinvented the wheel. Instantly I put my shoulder to it, but Pete pulled me roughly away, reinvented another wheel, attached the two of them to a bicycle frame that he had also reinvented and together we pedalled back down the learning curve as if the devil were after us. I looked over my shoulder. The devil was after us.

'Faster,' I screamed. Downwards we flew, past the lowest common denominators who backed away in fear, past the level playing field where someone was moving the goalposts, back towards the sanctuary of the old economy when, without warning, a vehicle appeared in front of us with flashing lights and blaring siren. We were going too fast to stop and we crashed slap bang into the ambulance at the foot of the cliff.

Pete was thrown from the bike, performed a double somersault and a single dead-cat bounce then lay as still as stone.

'A health professional, a health professional,' I screamed, 'my kingdom for a health professional.' I rushed to Pete's side and cradled his head in my hands.

'Pete, Pete,' I whispered urgently, 'use your communication skills to me.'

But it was no good. Pete's window of opportunity had closed for ever. He had reached his bottom line.

Pea neat

The gentle bumble bee, that harbinger of summer, visits a springtime blossom in much the same way as the Mongrel Mob visits a pensioner's house.

When a bee raids a sweet pea it perches on a small globe of petals just below the heart of the flower then buries its snout in nectar. The sweet pea appears to offer as much resistance to the theft as you would expect a sweet pea to offer, as much resistance indeed as most old people offer the Mongrel Mob.

But appearances deceive. When the bee lands it depresses the sweet pea's petals and cause them to separate. Through the slit between the petals a prong appears like a miniature rhino horn. The horn is tipped with yellow pollen as vivid as venom.

Just as when you visit the dentist you are so intent on what is going on in your mouth that you don't feel a thing as the wallet is removed from your back pocket, so the bee, intent on its nectar, doesn't notice as the pollen is smeared on its little furry buttocks. All unaware, it flies off to fertilise the next flower. It has become the winged inseminator. It is as if the elderly somehow managed to smear spermatozoa on the leather jackets of the Mongrel Mob, which is, I think, the point where that metaphor reaches the end of its useful life.

I discovered the cunning of the sweet pea during a traffic jam. Sweet peas proliferated in the lane in which I was jammed and I had nothing to do but study them. I was most impressed. The mechanism of the sweet pea seemed remarkably neat.

Such neatness in nature is just evolutionary ruthlessness. But neatness in people is folly. Neat people are prone to neurosis. I went to school with a boy who kept the same pencil case for seven years. His pencils were always sharpened. The coloured ones were held together with a rubber band and sorted for length. I guarantee that that boy now is either sad or mad. My money's on both.

For neat people seek to make life into a Fendalton drawing room, with floral wallpaper and all the furniture just so. But life isn't a Fendalton drawing room. It's more like an attic. The light doesn't work, you teeter on the floor joists, you can't find what you went there to fetch, you blunder into things you didn't go there to fetch, the things you didn't go there to fetch distract you and after a while you can't remember what you're doing there at all. Sometimes the roof permits you to stand to your full height and your spine unfurls with relief. You stride towards the future and headbutt a rafter.

Life's attic offers frustration, pain, puzzlement and occasional serendipitous delight. What it doesn't offer is neatness.

Don't expect neatness. The cosmos rarely does neatness. Heaven does neatness because God made heaven, but down here in real time there's a neatness shortage because God doesn't (a) care, (b) exist.

But sometimes, just sometimes, you catch a glimpse of how things ought to be, a hint of the neat and the just, a glimmer of light in the dark, chaotic attic.

Take, for example, the traffic jam where I observed the bee and the pea. The lane was blocked by a removal van. Its cab was empty. Several other cars were already waiting.

The driver of the leading car got out. I recognised him as my local electrician, a man who will respond to an emergency call at the drop of a chequebook. He must, by now, have changed almost every bulb in my house. I joined him in the sunny lane with its sweet proliferation of peas and bees. The removal man, he said, was down below and he pointed at a little cottage where a benign and shaggy mongrel leapt cheerfully at a white gate

The drivers in the traffic jam were mostly male and all frustrated. They sounded their horns like mastodons in rut. For a man in a car is a man with testosterone. At last he has the body God should have given him – 500 horsepower, a loud exhaust and a great big bonnet. He's king of the road, possums beware, hair in the wind and not to be messed with.

Behind their hot windscreens the stalled drivers fumed like bees in a jam jar. You could sense the hum of anger. They seethed with hatred for the removal man whose van blocked their rightful manly progress.

It was while I was studying the neatness of the sweet pea that Mr Inconsiderate emerged from the cottage. He sauntered into the sunlight as though the whole of time were his to spend. Horns greeted him. He looked up to see the line of traffic stretching back along the lane. To his credit he broke into a trot, reached the gate and bent to unlatch it. At this point the shaggy mongrel, boosted perhaps by the sun on its pelt and the unaccustomed activity, roused by the sight of a running removal man to memories of ancient hunts in distant lands, shook off the flimsy cloak of domesticity, reverted to the spirit of remote and feral wolves that roamed the winter wastes, and bit him on the buttock. The man yelped and we exulted.

It is unwise, I believe, to expect neatness, but there is no harm in rejoicing when it happens.

Love for lunch

Today I had lunch with a psychiatrist. This is not a behavioural pattern that I have previously exhibited – partly because I have known no psychiatrists but also because I have not thought well of their trade.

In twenty years of teaching I saw a number of disturbed children packed off to the couch. It rarely seemed to do them much good. In general I found that if anything mended the kids it was time and if nothing did then it was the legal system. My impression has always been that the brain is a dark, mysterious ocean and a large one, and that psychiatry is a blind fisherman in a very small boat.

Nevertheless this particular psychiatrist proved lively company at a party and we agreed to meet today in one of the more fashionable bits of downtown Christchurch. As I waited for her I sipped my beer and watched the crowd shuffling past in the winter sunshine. Perhaps it was the effect of my lunch-to-come but rather a lot of them looked mad.

The psychiatrist arrived fifteen minutes late, smiled like the sun, sat and did not apologise. I silently admired the ploy. We ordered gewürztraminer and a dish of bits of fish.

The conversation soared. We discussed meditation, Sanskrit vowels, chaos theory, sixteenth-century philosophy, twentieth-century philosophy, the growing prevalence of depression, the nature of joy, the popularity and value of Prozac and whether bacteria could be happy, all with a formidable sweep of lightly held knowledge to which I contributed several ums. I also refilled her glass twice.

And then we got onto love. Now I know a bit about love, and I said so. On the inside of my locker at school I had a photograph of Geoff Boycott. There was something about the way he held his bat, something about the sweet stretch of flannel over thigh pad that sang to my fourteen-year-old soul.

The psychiatrist looked quizzically at me over a slice of blackened monkfish but I persevered.

And then, I said, over the horizon came puberty, marching strongly and letting nothing obstruct it. And with it came love.

She asked me to describe the symptoms of love.

Moping, I said, featured prominently, along with self-pity, grinding despair, sulking, moonlit vigils and a curious addiction to reading and writing poetry. Would she like to hear some?

Despite the monkfish she shook her head with some vigour, reached for a prawn and asked if I still suffered these symptoms.

With a tolerant smile I explained that I had grown beyond such emotional intensity and had indeed been free of the effects of love for at least two years.

The prawn went South, pursued by a swig of gewürtz. 'And you call this love?' she asked.

I asked her what she would call it. She told me. There were several phrases. The least offensive was preoccupational emotive attachment.

Oh, I said, and I meant it to sting, but she swept on.

She acknowledged that to some extent psychiatrists were indeed fishing blind in a dark ocean, but there were some well lit-bits. You could, for example, dose people up with something mildly radioactive in the bloodstream, then get them to think certain types of thoughts and, with the help of a machine, study the bits of the head that were being used to think these thoughts. Every sense impression, she said, every feeling, every thought in the end is just a chemical reaction in the head, an influx of serotonin across the synaptic cavity or whatever. Now, she said, it was a curious coincidence but a colleague of hers was studying the sort of infatuation I had described. And her colleague had found a drug that seemed to cure it. The stuff was called – and I wrote this down to get it right – trifluoperazine.

She paused for effect and a morsel of snapper.

I said that I thought they should put trifluoperazine in the water supply. It would have spared us, for example, Donny Osmond or Boyzone. With trifluoperazine the Beatles today would be dodgy mechanics in a Liverpool backstreet, Tom Jones would be buying his own underwear, Winston Peters wouldn't get a single blue-rinse vote, Lady Chatterley could have got some knitting done, *Death in Venice* would have had a happy ending, someone would have punched Leonardo di Caprio and Lolita could have got School Cert.

'Yes indeed,' said the psychiatrist, and left me with the bill. It was $60.

Of chopping and sticking

It was not a successful evening. For a start I went grudgingly, because – well, you don't need the details. Let me just say that I went to say sorry. I had been in the wrong, of course, but that was all water under the bridge, or at least last night was meant to shove the water under the bridge and out into the great ocean of forgiveness. I planned, in short, to eat humble pie.

But I didn't eat humble pie. I ate Chinese. Chinese food does little for me. I have yet to find flavour in either noodles or rice. And then, of course, I got chopsticks.

Well now, I am as dextrous as the next man. I can tie my shoelaces, do up my flies and only on the very worst mornings do I confuse the activities. But I do not hold with chopsticks. Chopsticks are sticks. Sticks are bad cutlery.

Chopsticks do not chop and neither do they stick. If they were pointed you could at least spear the more substantial bits, but they aren't so you can't. And if a competition were held to discover the food least suited to consumption by chopsticks, rice would get the silver medal and noodles the gold.

We are supposed to be a tool-making species. Tool making is what has raised us into dominion over the beasts of the field and the birds of the air and the fishes of the sea. And when it comes to eating the beasts, birds and fishes, and in particular the smaller vegetables, the fork is a better tool than chopsticks. The spoon is a better tool than chopsticks. Indeed, virtually everything in your pockets is a better tool than chopsticks.

I do not mind other people using chopsticks. Though it may seem to me that those who are adept with chopsticks still use them mainly as shovels, and I find it impossible to imagine a worse design for a shovel, nevertheless, as I say, I have no quarrel with the users of chopsticks. Let them depart in peace.

Those I do have a quarrel with are those who expect me to use chopsticks. And these people are never those who were brought up with the things. Chinese restaurateurs are always delighted to fetch me my preferred weaponry.

No, the people who think it somehow right to use chopsticks to eat a dish that has been cut into little bits and laid on a bed of even littler bits, are people who were raised as I was raised with a silver-plated fork in the mouth. But when I call for a fork they look at each other in a mixture of shock and disdain and they tut. They consider me an oaf.

Now I do not deny oafdom. Oaf is a speciality of the house. But I fail to see why it should be considered a further black mark on my much marked escutcheon for me to wish to eat my food efficiently. It seems unreasonable. But reason, of course, doesn't come into it.

What does come into it is sycophancy, the belief that somehow one will ingratiate oneself with people from overseas by doing as they do. Wrong, of course. Restaurateurs of any breed don't give a fig how you eat their food. They give a fig only about whether you pay for it.

But the sycophants go further. By using chopsticks, they believe, one is leaving one's comfort zone and getting the authentic cultural experience.

Well phooey to that. For a start I like my comfort zone. I find it comfortable. But more significantly, I can think of no phrase more barren of meaning than authentic cultural experience. Authentic cultural experience means Disneyland. Authentic cultural experience means watching dances by grass-skirted people who, if you weren't paying them, would be wearing jeans and not dancing. Authentic cultural experience means bogus, artificial boredom.

All of which, of course, I didn't say. I was supposed to be behaving so I just bit my lip, grabbed a chopstick in each hand and spent a bitter evening scattering food. Hungry and angry make potent bedfellows. The water remains this side of the bridge and seems to have increased in volume.

Small stuff

There's a book called *Don't Sweat the Small Stuff.* I haven't read it because it's a self-improvement book and no self-improvement book has ever improved anyone except the author whom it often improves to the tune of several zillion bucks. But the title of this book intrigues me.

If, as I imagine, it advises the reader not to get swamped by trivia, but rather to keep his entrepreneurial eye forever trained on the horizon of opportunity where the big stuff roams, then I think it's hogwash. Big stuff sounds good but means little. 'Life,' said somebody, 'is just one damned thing after another.' Truth, such as it is, lies in the small stuff. It is always with us. The stuff like letter boxes.

When I bought my house it came with a letter box. It was a wooden letter box and a frail one but it did the job. It safely held the fizzing hate-mail and the accusations of dud grammar. It held the cheques I receive for writing stuff, and it even held a magnifying glass to read them with. The only thing my little letter box wouldn't hold on to was love letters. They dissolved like edible underwear. Perhaps they were written on edible underwear. Or perhaps the jealous dogs got to them first. But otherwise the letter box was sound.

Then one night its little roof blew off. I set to work repairing it with some fine wire nails and a dainty cabinet-maker's hammer, and in no time at all I had returned it to what it started as – which was several pieces of wood. They made good kindling.

Warm but letter boxless I took a catering-sized jam bucket and nailed it horizontally to a post.

Back indoors I wrote 'letter box' in my 'Things to do' book. The 'things to do' book is my way of handling the small stuff. When there's something I've got to do I write it in the book. When I've done it, I cross it out.

The aim of my life is to cross out all the small stuff. Then I can put my feet on the windowsill and gawp at the big stuff as God intended. But I never cross everything out. In fact my 'things to do' book reads like an inverse autobiography. My successes have all been crossed out but my failures stand tall. They're as persistent and shaming as genital warts. The letter box is one such.

Every day for two years my letter box has reproached me. 'You are idle,' it mutters, 'I am a jam bucket. Get a letter box. Everyone else has got a letter box.'

And because I've got a bad letter box, I notice that everyone else has got a good one. Fired by envy, I have become a connoisseur of letter boxes. I have noticed, for example, that three models dominate the suburban letter-box market – The Grim, The Gruesome and The Twee.

The Grim is the stalinist letter box. It is built of thin sheet metal painted anonymous cream. It's square as a shoebox, and smooth as a Martian's skull. It has a slot in its forehead and nothing else.

The Gruesome purports to be decorative and is normally to be found amid psychotically neat borders of flowering annuals. It consists of a metal stake sunk into the ground, a crossbar extending from the top of the stake and the kite-shaped letter box dangling from it like a corpse on a gallows.

The most popular design is the Twee. The Twee is wooden and looks like a miniature Swiss chalet. Under its steeply pitched eaves there's a triangular slot for newspapers, beneath that a compartment for letters with a flap at the back and beside that a compartment to house the lovely, bulky, promising parcels I never get.

And yesterday I bought a Twee. I wasn't looking for it. I chanced upon it outside one of those second-hand shops that sells dirty pieces of sadness. The price was right and the Twee was mine.

Back home I dug a hole and sank half a railway sleeper into it. I packed the earth around and trod it down. The thing stood firm. I placed the Twee on top of it and nailed it into place. I didn't hit my thumb and the Twee didn't split. I put lots of nails in. I shook it. It stood as solid as the Treasury. I tore the jam bucket from its mooring and threw it away.

Every five minutes I returned to check my letter box. Its firmness thrilled me. Its neatness delighted me. I kept opening and closing the flap for the joy that was in it. The postie arrived. She handed me a bill. I asked her to put it in the slot. She put it in the slot. I opened the flap and there was the bill. It was a fine moment. It was good small stuff.

In my 'things to do' book I crossed out 'letter box' and wrote 'pay bill'.

The stars above

'It is the stars, the stars above us, govern our conditions,' said the Earl of Kent in Act IV of *King Lear*, that same Earl of Kent, in case you are wondering, as wrote the astrology column for the *Elizabethan Women's Weekly*.

The great Earl comes to mind today because I have just had lunch with the Wise Woman. The Wise Woman, you must understand, is not the sort of hut-dwelling wise woman with a hooked nose, a black cat and a cupboardful of dried dog's-tongue, but a modern wise woman with a degree in something I don't understand and a PhD in something I seriously don't understand. She and I get on famously by disagreeing about everything. Our lunches resemble the Battle of the Somme.

Today, over a flat white sandwich and a long black coffee we amiably scratched at each other's eyes for a while then discussed why it is that we always disagree. Then Wise Woman asked me my star sign.

Across the rubble of plates, coffee cups and spent verbal bullets, I told her I was a Virgo. And that, it seemed, explained everything. Wise Woman told me that she always fought with Virgos. Virgos were, she said, dogmatic, sullen, intransigent, cantankerous, rebarbative – and a thesaurus-load of other adjectives, few of which I can remember but all of which combined to mean that she and a Virgo could simply never rub along.

I chewed over the abuse and my flat white sandwich. I sipped at my coffee and her long black words. For I had to admit that she had caught my character like a fly in amber. She had me sprawling on her pin. Perhaps because we were lunching in public and every wall sprouted ears, she had omitted some of my juicier failings, nevertheless she had said more than enough and every syllable of the reckoning was bang on and damning. Except for one teensy-weensy point. I am not a Virgo.

The Wise Woman is not the first of her kind to biff me with

the zodiac. In the last decade, 3281 women have asked me my star sign. In the same period the number of men who have done so is roughly 0.

I think I sniff a gender issue. I have always wanted a gender issue. Lots of people seem only to have to turn over the rock of any public matter to find a gender issue crawling underneath, but I have never found one before and I am excited. I have also recently lacked hate-mail.

Why is it, then, that so many women and so few men take an interest in the Zodiac, that sensible, talented women subscribe to the idea that lumps of cooling matter a squillion or so light years away affect our natures at birth? Why do they not recognise the self-evident truth that it is so much hocus-pocus?

For it is hocus-pocus, the most obvious drivel, the sort of 0900 driftwood that we feel the urge to cling to as we toss on the faithless seas of twentieth-century rationalism. Why can so many women not accept that all this business about Saturn in the ascendant makes as much sense as a Treasury forecast?

Furthermore, why can they not see that so many of the definitions of character in the astrologists' rantings are paradoxical? I, for example, am actually a Scorpio. (Don't tell me; you guessed as much. Well, you were right. Well done.) But at different times I have been told that Scorpios are extroverts and I have been told that they are shy. I have been told that Scorpios are secretive and that they are candid.

'Do I contradict myself?' asked Walt Whitman. 'Very well then,' continued old Walt, 'I contradict myself. I am large, I embrace multitudes.'

And that is exactly the point. We all embrace multitudes. We all know ourselves to be both heroes and cowards. We know ourselves to be both generous and selfish, wise and foolish, rash and cautious. Astrologers know it too and rely on it.

But how come so many women subscribe to it? Women, of course, are much nicer than men. They take an interest in other people while men take endless interest only in themselves.

Robert Graves began 'A Slice of Wedding Cake' with the

following question:

> Why have such scores of lovely, gifted girls
> Married impossible men?

Graves couldn't answer the question, and neither can I. But nor can I tell you why so many women seem to believe there are only twelve types of people. Is it, as the Wise Woman suggested, that women seek a system of belief that is not dominated by men? It might be so. Answers on a postcard, please, to my spiritual home c/o Aries the ram. (Yes, of course, you knew all along. Same birthday as Hitler, as it happens.)

Hot Toddy

I have never met the man who bears the name, but nor, I suspect, have many of the people who thronged Colombo Street on Tuesday. The banner headline in *The Press* announced 'In Todd They Trust' and 100,000 people took to the streets to prove the blasphemous punster right. The 100,000 came to greet and thank and celebrate a team of rugby players but mainly they came to gawp at Todd. They wore Todd masks and they prostrated themselves at his feet and they shouted his name.

Juliet, of course, thought names to be of no account.

'What's in a name?' she asked, 'That which we call a rose

By any other name would smell as sweet.'

For romantic reasons Juliet was hardly neutral on the subject of names, but anyway she was wrong. We wouldn't plant a rose called skunk.

Names matter. When Adam was granted dominion over the birds of the air and the fishes of the sea and everything else that crept, ran, flew, swam or just grew, the first thing he did was to name them. Names enable us to grasp the world.

If we do not know a person's name we are at a disadvantage. Without a name we have to deal with the thing itself rather than the label and we find that hard. But there would be few houses in New Zealand that Todd Blackadder could walk into to find that no one knew his name.

And what a name. I know little about rugby and I care less, but I know a good name when I see one.

Todd is strong. Its single syllable leaves nothing to debate. It's all consonants and consonants are the bones of words. Where vowels merely slide from the mouth, consonants do things. The letters T and D are plosives. To say them we have to curl the tongue against the roof of the mouth and then slap it down with a gust from a throat like a possum's hiss.

No girl could be called Todd. Girls' names may begin with T

but they taper into open vowels or a lingering sinuous y – Tina, Teresa, Tracy.

The word Todd suggests much. It echoes plod, and the image of an old-fashioned rural policeman, unspectacular, honest and earnest. But it holds hints of toddle too, and toddler, the innocent child, the one who enjoys life but needs guidance, is unstable but enthusiastic and generous and wide-eyed in a manner that stretches our hearts. No wonder the women swoon.

Though Todd is good, Blackadder is better. Like Todd, Blackadder is a clusterbomb of consonants. It packs another bunch of D's, coupled now with the explosive B and the cackle of the K.

The rhythm of the whole name throws the emphasis onto the word 'black' and no word in the language carries more negative connotations. Black is the absence of light, is the colour of spite. Black thoughts, black deeds, black looks, the black heart of the blackguard. Then add the adder. An adder is a viper, a venomous snake. (It used to be called a nadder but the n migrated, perhaps because it was scared.) After the strong stress of 'Black', the double syllable of adder rattles like a threat. Come no nearer, I've got fangs.

Every component of the name is right. Each verbal building block is Anglo-Saxon and forthright as a punch. No latinate abstractions, no sliding doubtful vowels.

And now Todd Blackadder has been promoted to a position more eminent than that of prime minister. And the people have embraced him.

For in a world of change where nothing is as once it was Todd Blackadder returns us to certainty. With his giant placidity, like the Port Hills on Prozac, his lopsided smile, the lips pulled to one side by what looks to be a duelling scar on the cheek, his monosyllabic eloquence in which there seems to be no editing between heart and mouth, he resurrects the old New Zealand from a sea of cappuccino. Rugged as the landscape, resolute as a pioneer, liking his going tough, giving no fig for money but everything for honour, he thinks a canapé is something you shelter under to watch the rugby. He's as New Zealand as a roast. His heart is as big as his boots and his boots are size 17.

As I said at the start I do not know Todd Blackadder so I do not know if what I have said about him is true. But I think people think it is true and I think that they think it is good and so it is both true and good.

A good old story

Good stories are common as sparrows. But stories of good are less common, and stories of good which are also good stories are as rare as the kakapo. But such a story has just hatched. It is the story of Mr Cronje. In case you missed the news, Mr Cronje was captain of the South African cricket team, an outfit renowned for its frivolity. Mr Cronje added his bit to the fun by having a face carved from the sort of concrete that makes the Christchurch Town Hall such a pretty building. He also wore the permanently blue chin of a man whose masculinity is not to be doubted.

Mr Cronje was renowned for playing hard but fair. Hard but fair is normally a euphemism meaning nasty and keen to cheat. But in Mr Cronje's case it seemed to mean what it says. Under his leadership the South African cricket team has spent the last few years trampling on the tracheas of their opponents and thereby bringing great joy to themselves and to a lot of South Africans. Mr Cronje expressed his joy by scowling, thus giving further joy. He and his team seemed not to know self-doubt and so thrashed teams like England who justifiably ooze it. Sports teams who believe that sport matters and who believe that they are going to win, win. The meek do not inherit the world cup.

But, as we all know, Mr Cronje no longer captains South Africa. He tossed away a jewel worth more than his tribe. He sold his soul for a mess of pottage, in the form of a few thousand dollars from an Indian bookmaker. The police got wind of the deal and whispered a word or two, it seems, to the South African Cricket Board who in turn whispered some questions to Mr Cronje.

Mr Cronje denied wrongdoing. He denied it with vigour. He denied it repeatedly. His denials were blazoned across headlines across the world. And although people love to see the prominent tumble, and although people tend to believe that there is no smoke without a bloody great bonfire somewhere, I suspect that most people doubted that Mr Cronje had done anything wrong, because although Mr Cronje seemed a dull man, he seemed also to be an incorruptible man. It was unthinkable that he should have done anything so venal and foolish.

Well, the unthinkable should always be thought. Scepticism, especially in matters of power and money – which are synonyms – is a virtue. And so, of course, it transpired. Mr Cronje had indeed done it. He had taken the moolah. Why he took it in one sense remains a mystery, for he was prospering and the sum given was comparatively trivial, but he took it. In the end I suspect he was just greedy. You and I are of course immune to greed, but Mr Cronje, it seems, is not. Let's have fun casting stones at him.

But the greed is less interesting than the way the story unfolded. From what I can gather, Mr Cronje got walloped by the middle-of-the-night blues. For it seems that after a day of denials and of being followed by photographers and other crustacea, none of whom had the least apparent effect on him, Mr Cronje went home and went to bed.

And bed got him. What the press could not do and what Mr Ali Bacher of the South African Cricket Board could not do, bed did. For Mr Cronje was not in bed alone. He lay wide-eyed and sleepless with a small voice. The voice urged him to own up.

He was faced with the dilemma which faced Macbeth. Should he ignore the voice and harden his heart and plough deeper into the trough of amoral success or should he come clean and purge the bosom of that perilous stuff which weighed upon the heart? Macbeth chose the former. Mr Cronje, bless him, chose the latter.

At three in the morning he rose from his bed and he rose as a man and he telephoned Mr Bacher and pronounced himself guilty. How did he feel when he did so? He felt cleansed. By admitting his weakness he became strong. He knew as he owned up that he could face every stone that you or I could cast at him. He could stand before the baying mob in the impenetrable armour of honesty. He had hurt himself. We could no longer hurt him.

Mr Cronje is apparently a devout Christian but I don't believe that matters.

For Christianity, like all religions, merely acknowledges the human condition and supplies a framework of words and metaphors to accommodate it. Christianity did not invent good or evil or conscience or honesty or confession. These things are as old as people. And to see them work out again and again in human affairs, always the same, always the old old story, revives one's faith in a sorry world, reminds us that there is no guilt so great that it cannot be confessed, nor any crime so wicked that it cannot be forgiven, and confirms that, beneath the tat and triumphal emptiness of a society mad for sport and washing machines, certain truths hold true as stone.

Yurt and yak

Why do we surround ourselves with stuff? Now is the season of stuff, of course, almost all of it dreadful stuff, combination-barbecue-tool type stuff, or matching-nail-clipper-and-shampoo-set stuff, the sort of stuff that will be garage sale fodder within months. A few more months and it will go permanently to ground where it will leach nasties to poison our progeny for the next few millennia, but no one cares much about that for obvious reasons. And anyway that's not the sort of stuff I mean.

The sort of stuff I mean is the art stuff. By art stuff I mean the pretty stuff, the expressive stuff, the stuff we display on walls or shelves to make our homes, well, nicer.

The ancient nomads didn't go in for art stuff. They loaded the yak with the yurt and the saucepans but they biffed the Titian on the fire because it served no purpose. But as soon as nomads settled down, as soon as they found themselves a cave in one of the nicer suburbs, they started painting reindeer on the walls. They became civilised, which etymologically means nothing more than that they lived in towns. With civilisation came the art stuff. And it came to stay. We modern hunter-gatherers have ditched the yak and the yurt, and we go hunting only in supermarkets, but we've underlined the gathering. We call it collecting. I wonder if we're wise.

The people who gave me lunch and bubbly yesterday collect a species of crockery called Carltonware. It's chunky fifties stuff painted a distinctive bile green. The details are picked out in lung-pink and vomit-yellow. They've got cabinets crammed with the stuff. Whenever I visit them I stare at the stuff as I would at a butcher's window.

These people also collect paintings. Barely an inch of their walls is bare. They have lived in the same house for thirty years and their collection of art stuff has grown around them like a coral reef. They do not mean to move. The prospect of shifting all that stuff from the walls to the back of a yak would daunt the toughest nomad. Easier and wiser to stay and gather.

I don't go in for visual art stuff, though I did once buy a painting of a cabbage at the opening of an exhibition where champagne abounded. I have the painting still and hate it.

But I do go in for books. I love to own books. Though I read few books twice, I have filled every shelf in my house with books, have had more shelves made and have filled those too. My books surround me like a cocoon. When I run my finger along the backs of my books they feel like the ribcage of an old familiar lover. Visit my shelves and you will learn much about me.

And that, perhaps, is the nub of the matter. The art stuff we put on our walls and our shelves, the stuff we cram into display cabinets, anything from cats in brandy balloons to the works of Dostoevsky, announces something about us. We paste our tastes and tendencies upon our walls to produce a cradle of self in which to live. It is both a vanity and a reassurance, a bulwark against a world that cares too little about us.

But what will happen when I go to the eternal landfill? Someone presumably will go through my books, keeping a few perhaps but selling off the bulk of them too cheaply to someone who trades in the unwanted chattels of the dead. My collection will disintegrate like the atoms of my flesh. My books will scatter to second-hand bookshops where people like myself will pick them over, buying the pieces that suit their image of themselves and will shelve them, to build up their own collection, their own vain expression of self, like a stork selecting twigs to build a nest.

Perhaps the nomads were right. A yurt and a yak and a wide wide sky.

Emotion in aspic

When your grandmother died did you go through her things, the remnants of a lived life, and find, tucked away under some linen perhaps, or clasped within the covers of a book, a little bundle of letters tied with pink ribbon? Did you then gently untie that frayed and faded ribbon, feeling like a trespasser as you did so, slide a letter from an envelope, flatten the creases in the paper that time had made frail, and read in faded ink the ancient words of love? No, nor did I.

But I would have liked to do so. For I relish letters. Letters are gifts. More honest than photographs, letters are emotion in aspic. Letters are as personal as touch. They can be held, treasured, folded in pockets and purses, sniffed and kissed, or torn in two and burned.

Other people's letters are a voyeur's delight. Published collections of the letters of eminent people sell well, because they are the best form of autobiography. Good letters sing with honesty. In letters you do not find the evasions, omissions and half-truths that make autobiographies into works of fiction. No one polishes a letter for posterity, except, that is, W.B. Yeats who sometimes asked for his letters back so that he could amend them. Yeats was nuts.

Of the letters I have received over the years only one has changed my life. But of the thousands of others, many have given joy.

What pleases so about letters is that they are links to a past, like the streamers thrown to shore when a liner leaves port. But now, I fear, the letter is threatened. E-mail is taking over. E-mail is a priceless business tool, but it lacks romance. It has the permanence and elegance of a hamburger.

Because e-mail is so easy, swift and cheap, people use it too much. Most e-mail messages are blurts, ill-spelt, ill-chosen and ill-considered spasms of words, as significant as sneezes. While a good letter is a butterfly, netted and gassed some distant summer and now pinned forever under glass, an e-mail is a blowfly, common, black, ugly, dirty and dead.

But in a world without butterflies a man must clutch at blowflies. Today I received an e-mail from Ben who is exiled in Belgium. Living in Belgium is doing it tough. Belgium is all cream and hideous dolls in national dress and bourgeoisie and smothering boredom relieved only by a horrific subculture of fat pederasts. Ben has not lived abroad before and is homesick. He has been torn up by the roots. He is pining for Ashburton. It's that serious.

He tells me that a day without e-mail from down under is a dire day, that he needs a fix of contact with his past to buoy him through his present. E-mail is his lifeline.

His words took me back. When I left university some time around the end of the nineteenth century I somehow fetched up in Spain and love.

I soon fell out of love but stayed in Spain. I was not homesick but, surrounded by a foreignness of which I was no part, I felt the need for contact from my elsewhere. E-mail was not yet a glint in Bill Gates' eye. I longed for airmail letters whose blue and red edging is the sexiest colour I know. An empty letter box stung.

With springwater clarity I remember one afternoon when I went back to a flat on the thirteenth floor in Calle de Felisa Gale, a flat from which I had been kicked out after a spat over domestic chores. Calle de Felisa Gale lay on the far side of the city but a couple of months after leaving I walked the 5 miles back there in the hope of letters. I found a dozen fat airmail envelopes awaiting me. It was like stumbling on the end of the rainbow. On the return trek across the city, I read as I walked. Engrossed in words, I crossed Avenida Generalissimo Mola and was hit a sidelong blow by a yellow Fiat. It spun me out of the past and into the gutter of now. But I cherish letters still.

And the letter that changed my life? I can quote it in full. I had written in mawkish self-pity to a friend in Paris. The reply, 'Know what you are and be it, creep.'

Seduced

I've been seduced again, thank God. My seducer was E.B. White the essayist, Elwyn perhaps to his wife and family, but E.B. to those of us who read him. And old E.B. of whom I have never seen a photograph but whom I imagine wearing old-man tweeds and wise-man glasses, seduced me by telling me of his chickens. He wrote of Golden Wyandottes and Speckled Orpingtons and I was sold.

I have been seduced by chickens before. Thirty years ago my brother bought two battery hens at an auction. They wore a few anaemic feathers, and their legs wobbled. He took the sad birds home, fed them grain and grass and freedom and within weeks they stood proud and brown, birds to daunt a dog, strutting fowl with combs as dramatic as lipstick on a courtesan.

Fired by the memory and by old E.B. I resolved to start the century with chickens. From there I might move on to pigs, geese and a goat. From a woman of the soil I borrowed *Self Sufficiency*, a book that spoke in entertaining terms of how to rear a pig, feed it skimmed milk, nurse it through the illnesses of piglet-hood and kill it. And then, having killed it, how to saw around its anus, hack its innards out and hang its hocks and hams amid the chimneypiece to smoke their way to bacon. I crossed pig off my list. I have a gas fire.

At the same time I had also to acknowledge that I am no farmer. I am as rural as Woody Allen. Because my hands are pudgy-white and I am nervous of cattle I would be unwise to plunge into animal husbandry. I should enter into it with caution as into a hard-hat area – although I do sometimes wonder whether anyone in the history of hard hat areas has ever known a brick to land on his hard hat – and my means of entry, my introduction to the self-sufficient life, would be chooks. Their needs, I read, are few.

Having surfed the internet for chicken-house designs, I emerged from under my house with a hammer, a box of ancient nails and enough discarded timber to build an ark and as I lugged it all up the garden I strove to remember what I had learned in woodwork classes thirty years ago. I recalled my nonagenarian teacher telling me not to waste wood because it didn't grow on trees, and I recalled triumphantly carrying home my first successful project and being hugely praised for it – so well-made was that chopping board that I believe my mother still uses it – but otherwise I recalled nothing.

Five minutes into henhouse construction it all came back. What came back was the joy of swinging the hammer squarely onto a thumbnail. The only sensation I know to match it is stubbing a toe. In both instances the pain lurks offstage for perhaps two seconds. That seems the worst moment because you know with terrified bewilderment that the pain will come. But it is not the worst moment. The worst moment is when the pain comes. It surges with a ferocity that makes you yearn for amputation. I clenched the thumb between my thighs, then held it as far away from me as possible, then ran around the garden shouting. The dogs joined in the game.

But I persevered and slowly a chookhouse grew. It held perches and nest boxes and sliding doors that sometimes slid, and a ramp leading into a pen of straw and other pens of grass – the Balfour system which I had read about. Above the pen stands a plum tree which in autumn will bombard the chickens with their lunch. And all was dog-proof too, as I confirmed by placing a bone in the middle of it.

One day later, closely attended by a brace of dogs and studied from afar by a cat, I eased the lid off a banana box and released three hens, the offspring of a Rhode Island Red and something equally traditional, into the surprise of a new world. Within minutes they were scratching through the straw for grain. Within hours they had eaten the grass. Within a day they had strutted, clucked and pecked their way into my heart. I lack the space here to say how. Perhaps I also lack the words to convey the deep contentment of a chicken's brooping, or the iridescence of the black-green feathers on its back or the spearing accuracy of its beak guided by a round primeval eye.

This week I got my first egg, laid as neat and clean as any supermarket egg on a hollow of straw. It was warm. I fried it in butter. It was a fine egg. It cost me $35 for chicken wire, $9.95 for tin-snips to cut the wire, $8 to replace the scissors that failed to cut the wire, $6 for a bag of wheat, $12 for layer pellets, $7 for straw, $20 for the hens themselves, ten minutes a day for tending to their needs and two hours a day for leaning on the fence to admire them. And I got, I reckon, a bargain.

Moving bad things

Bad things don't go away. You can put them in a cupboard but when you move house the bad things will still be in the cupboard. And they will have got worse.

So it was that Tom and Cathy – they asked me not to use their real names which are Patrick and Jeanette – discovered that they owned six tangerine-coloured Indonesian floating candles, a roll of slug tape, floral placemats, a teapot with a wicker handle, ancient secateurs and a dead microwave as big as a tomb. Tom and Cathy knew exactly what to do with stuff that no one could possibly want. They held a garage sale.

By inviting friends to contribute items they amassed a cornucopia of tat. I warned Cathy that I knew of a man who held a garage sale and had most of the best items stolen. She appointed me official security guard.

The sale began at 8.30 so I arrived promptly to guard it at 10. The house was humming. Tom was sizzling sausages, and cutting up onions. Everyone else was cutting deals. Well-dressed women were leaving with armfuls of *Home and Garden* magazines from the mid-nineties. The teapot with the wicker handle had gone. Students had snapped up the orange armchairs. Those chairs will now be sitting on a verandah getting wet and leaking stuffing. The students also took the microwave.

Stock was running low so despite my security role I was put to work. I carried out from the house a spice rack with two jars, a soap dish shaped like a fish, a leather Jim Beam bottle-holder, a wire fruit bowl, black women's shoes 'worn only once' – presumably because the wearer broke her ankle – a floral lampshade, an iron with stains, two rolls of dissimilar wallpaper, a set of earphones with cobwebs and torn padding, a hardened paint roller, a mug-tree, a golf trolley without wheels or handle and a watercolour print of flowers which I dropped for aesthetic reasons. The glass shattered. I put the shards on a table, then sat on a wall to eat sausages and catch thieves.

The goods were not good. Yet somehow, somewhere, someone had thought they needed to be invented, manufactured and distributed to the waiting world. Now, after a life of neglect, they sat in a suburban driveway, like orphans begging for a home. Little of the stuff was useful, and none of it beautiful. But it sold.

For four hours the driveway was rarely empty. People of all descriptions came and went. Second-hand dealers swooped, assessing the tat, snatching a piece of it, halving the price, moving on, collecting a trailerful. They must have been up at dawn to plan the best route round the city of classified ads.

Whole families came, with girls in pony-tails and boys in cargo pants. Men came on bicycles and didn't take off their helmets. Studious people turned the china over to check the maker's stamp. A local celebrity bought the paint roller for 50 cents, and discussed classical music over a sausage.

Commerce dwells in our blood. Few people bought things because they needed them. They bought them because they were cheap. Despite a voice in my head I found I couldn't resist a bottle of aftershave I wouldn't use, a briefcase I didn't need and the ancient secateurs.

The students came back. The microwave had spat arcs of blue plasma at them. They spent their refund on a mirror and the Jim Beam stand.

Time and again the tables emptied and the sellers, drunk with the joy of trading, scurried to their houses to retrieve more detritus. Digging out stuff turned out to be like vomiting: there was always a little more to come. Unused council rubbish bags marked 'not to be sold' sold instantly. Someone bought a Thai Airlines promotional handbag.

The floating candles had been a gift – presumably from the blind to the unloved. Tom asked the mature woman who bought them whether she was planning a romantic evening. She snorted. A woman in pink bought the statue which I have been asked to describe as African in case the relatives who brought it back from South America read this. She paid $4.

A man picked up the largest shard of glass from the picture I had broken. He turned it over, studied it and for one thrilling moment I thought he was going to make an offer. But he bought the slug tape instead.

It was a happy gentle morning. In four hours over 600 untaxed black-market dollars changed hands, almost all of it in coins. Hundreds of ugly things moved home. The last rites were delivered by a chap from a church who ate two cooling sausages and took away everything unsold for nothing.

When I got home I snipped at the hedge with my secateurs. They broke. I put the aftershave in the briefcase, and the briefcase in a cupboard.

Messing

It is all very well to mess with ourselves, but when we mess with nature we get problems.

For example, my mate Pat's got a radioactive cat. The beast developed a growth in its thyroid so the vet injected it with a substance that makes it glow in the dark. I should feel sympathy for the mog but, as with most misfortune, I find it funny, and besides it's one of those cats that expresses affection by biting.

The vet isolated the thrumming cat for a few days in a lead-lined cage but now that it's back at home it has to be locked out at night so that it doesn't sneak onto Pat's pillow and make him grow a second head. So instead it wanders luminously over the neighbour's roof, warping the corrugated iron and alarming the passing drunks.

Each morning Pat scans the yellowing vegetation of his garden with a Geiger counter, finds the beast and lets it into the house. But if he falls asleep on the sofa and wakes with the thing on his lap he has to take a two-hour shower and check his sperm count. One million and one, one million and two...

Now luminosity hinders hunting, so I doubt if Pat's cat at present is much good at catching birds, but I expect it gives them a fright. My own cat, however, which to my knowledge has never been radioactive, is in mid-season hunting form. Only this afternoon I found it torturing a sparrow with the sort of glee that I find it hard to like. Had there been any point in doing so I would have rescued the sparrow but I was already too late by a matter of several organs. The sparrow still tried to flutter away but aerodynamically it was a gone possum.

Five minutes later the cat brought me the tubular remains and rubbed against me in search of praise which I refused to give. Indeed, right now if my cat developed a dicky thyroid I don't think I'd fork out for the plutonium.

On the day I acquired my three chickens the cat stalked them.

Ten metres from the coop it slunk down into that low-bellied crawl which it learned from David Attenborough, and then spent the best part of an hour sneaking up on the unwitting chooks across the lawn. On my lawn that's no great feat. In a recent gale my dustbin blew away – not much to my regret because its lid had always stuck and now I had the excuse to buy a green deluxe model from The Warehouse – but as soon as I'd replaced it I stumbled on the old bin which had been hiding in the depths of the lawn.

So the cat in the lawn was like a pedestrian in Manhattan, but still it stole towards the chickens with extraordinary caution, moving each limb separately with a rapt and sinuous malice. Eventually it parted the grass at the edge of the coop, beheld the chooks clearly for the first time, saw that each bird was twice its size, stared at them in a wild surmise then promptly lost interest.

Since then two chickens have gone broody, which means that they spend their days trying to hatch the eggs they haven't got. If the one active chook lays an egg the broodies fight over it until I take it away. Broody chooks don't lay and since they've nothing to rear I was keen to snap them from their broodiness. Pat of the luminous cat told me that one way to do it was to toss the chickens into the air.

So every day for the last two weeks I've tossed my chickens. As I reach into the nesting boxes the broodies swell like puffer fish, cluck weakly in protest and peck at my hands, but once they've been tossed and have fluttered back to earth and stood for a while to reorder brains the size of paper-clips, they suddenly remember that they are chickens and peck madly at grain and grass and swig beaksful of water. Then they go back to their brooding till it's tossing time again.

Confronted with the failure of the tossing gambit I consulted the Internet. In ten minutes I had found a website called Fowlnews where I joined the hugely popular 'Poultry Information Exchange' and posted my problem on its virtual bulletin board. I expect you saw it.

Anyway, within the hour I had received several bits of virtual advice. Among them came an e-mail from a chicken-fancier known as Buzz from Wisconsin. Buzz told me that it is sometimes possible to snap chickens out of broodiness by scaring them. I'm going to borrow Pat's cat.

PS. I thank the correspondent who asked whether my phrase 'black women's shoes' in a recent column was the result of illiteracy or racism. I would love to plead illiteracy but I must admit to racism. I should of course have written 'Afro-American women's shoes'. I apologise to all whom I offended.

The right side and the rest

Last week I went to a Catholic wedding. The groom's family and friends on the right-hand side of the cathedral were Catholic. The bride's on the left were not. The priest intoned prayers or whatever and from the right-hand side came responses as involuntary as breathing. From us on the left, nothing.

Catholicism fascinates me. As a child I went into churches only on holiday, when my mother would drag me round the flagged and cold interior of some cathedral to look at I don't know what and I would sulk and pout and beg to be taken out and given ice cream.

At state primary school we used to say a prayer at the end of the day after we had put the chairs on the desk. The prayer were just noise. At secondary school religion meant 'Onward Christian Soldiers' once a week in assembly just before the soccer results.

I was as secular as an animal but at university I had a lapsed Catholic friend called Dave. He was fun to drink with. Late in the evening a diabolical streak emerged in him. He did dangerous and memorable things that made me laugh.

Then one evening when I went to fetch him he looked mournfully at me and said he wasn't coming out. God, he said, had held him down in a chair and made him chose between good and evil, between the pub and the Lord. He had chosen the Lord. I mocked. I argued. I wheedled. I said he had been brainwashed. He said he was sorry but he wouldn't budge.

For weeks I behaved appallingly. Whenever I saw Dave I would heckle him. He bore it all and continued to be kind to me. Nothing angered him. That angered me. Eventually the road between us fell into disuse.

A while later I read *Brideshead Revisited*. And then I read *The Power and the Glory*. And though I knew I could never enter Dave's world I thought I could begin to see something of how it worked.

A few years later I went to work in Spain. Of the two Catholic cathedrals in the city one was dark, medieval and empty. The other was built in the eighteenth century around a pillar on which the Virgin Mary was supposed to have appeared to a saint. El Pilar lay on my way home from work and I took to dropping in. Passing the crippled beggars at the door, I would stroll with hundreds of other everyday people through the echoing aisles. Sometimes I would be surprised by a service happening in a side chapel and I would scurry past. But also sometimes I would buy a candle, always paying more than I needed to, and would light it and place it on the rack by the door

Behind the huge and jewelled altar a part of the original holy pillar was exposed so that people could kiss it. A constant queue of men and women stood waiting their turn. I joined them only once. The pillar was cold black marble. As I laid my lips on it I felt like a fraud.

That Christmas Eve I ate shellfish with a girl called Maria and then we went to midnight mass. We went not to the popular Pilar but to La Seo, the medieval palace of gloom. When the choir came up the nave with candles I shivered. My shivering rocked the pew.

I woke up in a bed in Maria's flat where a drunken doctor who had been summoned from a Christmas party was injecting my buttock with a medieval-looking syringe. Apparently I had collapsed during the service and writhed on the flagstones squealing. Men had had to carry me out to a taxi. I spent Christmas and Boxing Day and the day after Boxing Day throwing up bile and being injected. The doctor said it was probably the shellfish. When I got better I facetiously said it was God. He had struck down the infidel, I said.

I still go into Catholic churches. I am surprised by what Larkin called the hunger in himself to be more serious. I have heard all sorts of stories from lapsed Catholic friends about indoctrination, about guilt, about cruel nuns, but I wish I knew the dogmatic certainty of the Catholic faith if only as something to kick against.

I envy the faithful the Latin mass, censers and chasubles – whatever a chasuble is – communion and confessional, a ritual sanctified by thousands of years of use. But however much I might think that I want to sit on the right-hand side of the cathedral I shall only ever sit on the post-war baby-boomer left, the sceptical product of my age and upbringing, barren of mysticism, impatient for ice cream and the bright light of the mortal day outside.

The sell-by chef

My career as a television chef began in what passes for a supermarket in the seaside town of Obscurity where I was living between jobs. A television director, scouting for talent with a hand-held camera, stopped me at the checkout.

'Show us your basket,' he ordered. I tilted the red plastic container towards the lens, and displayed the ordinary foodstuffs from which I would conjure something extraordinary by way of dinner.

'Zoom in on the bread,' said the director and the simplicity of a toast-slice loaf filled the frame. 'I like it,' said the director. 'Talk us through it.'

With a hint of a lisp and a smile that beguiled, I explained how bread which had reached its sell-by date was sold at half-price. 'Boys,' said the director, 'we've got a title.'

And thus 'The Sell-By Chef' was born and the gas-flame of my fame was lit.

I led the crew home where they gasped at the unadorned ruggedness of my kitchen. I whistled the dogs to clean the bench then said simply, 'Ladies and gentlemen, let's cook.'

'Just roll 'em,' screamed the director to the cameraman as I prised the plastic tab from the bread bag in a manner so practised that it looked easy and flicked it across the kitchen like the schoolboy that at heart I am and which I make no effort to conceal from the camera.

'Priceless,' said the director, 'they'll lap it up.' I delved into the bag, tossed the crust to the dogs, then held a rectangular slice up close to the camera's inquisitive lens. 'Bread,' I said.

Television is a visual medium. I gave not another word of explanation, as, with enthralling slowness, I folded the bread into the palm of my hand and closed my fist around its textured white heart, squeezing until a little tongue of compressed dough oozed like hesitant toothpaste from the interstice between my crunched pinkie and my palm.

'Sexy,' drooled the director.

Slowly, like a bud unfolding, I opened my hand to show what had once been a slice of aging bread now compressed into something little larger than a golf ball with the texture of white playdough. Shreds of bread adhered to the skin of my hand.

'Dwell on it,' screamed the director to the cameraman. 'It's the perfect cover. For the book of the series.'

I nodded. He and I shared a wavelength.

I flung the golf-ball to the dogs then hauled towards me the plump hump of my toaster. With a rattlesnake speed that took the camera by surprise I dropped a brace of slices into the slots and depressed the moulded black plastic tongue on the toaster's flank.

The camera tilted to my face. I smiled enigmatically. 'Ease,' I said, 'that's what it's all about, ease and zen. A great cook exudes calm. Everything is one. We are what we eat. Now come with me.' Without pausing I led them into the other room where I swept newspapers imperiously from the sofa, and lowered the cameraman onto a whoopee cushion.

Its resonant fart drew gales of delight from the director. 'You are the child in all of us,' he exulted, 'every mother's son, every young girl's bad-boy lover. You are *it*.'

I was the first to smell the smoke. But I refused to run. In the kitchen I grasped the handle of a fork which protruded from the depths of solidified fat in the frying pan. The pan rose, as if reluctant to relinquish ownership, then the fork came away with the sound of a boot leaving mud and the pan fell back onto the hob.

I plunged the fork into a flaming slice, tossed the bread in the air, caught it, patted it from hand to hand, laid it on the bench, then did it again. Thick was the butter that I smeared on each slice. It melted instantly into the charred bread. Thick, too, was the raspberry jam. I handed a slice to the director. The camera stayed with me, dwelt on my mouth.

'Pain flambé au framboise,' I said, quietly, understatedly, and I sank my young and perfect teeth into its smoking, butter-rich heart.

Qualified nonsense

The average age of teachers is rising because many young teachers are leaving the profession. They are leaving because the job keeps changing and the workload growing. They are leaving because the joy has gone out of it. And they are leaving because they have to spend more time with paper and less time with kids.

The Ministry of Education and my old friends the New Zealand Qualifications Authority have done their best, and are continuing to do their best, to make things worse. Most recently they have changed yet again the system of qualifications in schools.

A couple of years ago the Ministry and the NZQA preached the pleasures of unit standards. Unit standards were silly things, but I am sure you recall hearing a lot about them. They would produce a seamless education system. Millions of dollars and truckloads of consultants were tipped into their development. Many people said at the time that unit standards would never work for conventional school subjects such as English, but the bureaucrats pooh-poohed the critics.

Now, you may recall not hearing quite so much about unit standards in recent months. This is because, astonishingly, the Ministry of Education and the NZQA have now admitted the truth which everyone else could see from the start. To a fanfare of fiercely embarrassed silence, they have dumped unit standards for schools. Unit standards remain, I believe, for vocational training, but schools will see them no more. I have heard no word of apology for the millions of your dollars and my dollars which have been wasted, nor for the thousands of hours that teachers put into preparing for them.

A couple of years ago I predicted the demise of unit standards. When I did so, a certain Dr Blackmur, head honcho of the NZQA, took time off from his arduous schedule to write me some stinging abuse. Now Dr Blackmur has taken the plane back to his native

Australia – something which he did remarkably often at your and my expense during his tenure – and I have left it too late to crow.

In such a hurry was Dr Blackmur to leave the rubble of his former empire that he barely had time to clutch his golden handshake, a trivial sum amounting to little more than three years' salary for a teacher. I was caught out by the good doctor's departure because his contract with the NZQA had not actually expired. He left because his conditions of employment had changed. Poor dear. Perhaps the new conditions required him to do some good.

If every teacher followed Dr Blackmur's example and left when their conditions of employment changed, our schools would be empty. For the only constant in schools is change. And now things are to change again.

Instead of unit standards, schools must now adopt a new system called the National Certificate of Educational Achievement. The NCEA is being rushed in for the sound educational purpose of saving face.

Several terms exist to describe the NCEA. One of these is compromise. Another is hotchpotch. A third is bastard. For the NCEA is what you get from mating the traditional system of examinations with the collapsed idea of unit standards. Inevitably the child is illegitimate.

The NCEA includes internally assessed things called achievement standards. Achievement standards are essentially unit standards under a new name, except that they come with grades attached rather than a mere pass or fail.

The Ministry of Education has decided that the NCEA will take effect in schools very soon. And having so decided, they have sent out questionnaires inviting teachers to comment on the details. Over the years I have seen many such questionnaires from the Ministry. Each effectively said, 'Dear Teacher, we have decided to bomb your house. Would you rather we used cluster bombs or laser-guided missiles? Please reply on the enclosed form. We do value your opinion.'

I do not have the space to explain in detail why the NCEA is ill-considered, unwieldy and wrong. All I will say for now is that if the NCEA were a building it would collapse. Its foundations are rotten. The NCEA is built on the belief that all subjects from boiler-making to philosophy can and should be assessed by the same system; and that when we teach children we are simply preparing them for jobs; and that failure is bad for children; and that a subject like English can be divided into chunks which can be learned, tested and ticked off the list. All of these beliefs are fallacies.

Furthermore, the whole edifice is founded on the eduspeak of the semi-literate new curriculum and the qualifications framework.

What should happen is for the ministry to gulp down its pride and acknowledge that the best way to assess most subjects is by external exams. We all know that exams are imperfect, but at least they are simple, they are fair and they allow teachers to get on with teaching. But that won't happen.

Like unit standards the NCEA will eventually collapse, but it will take a while and by then it will have driven yet more teachers from the classroom.

My advice to those teachers is simple. Join the bureaucracy. You won't have to do anything useful. You'll toss dollars around like autumn leaves. You'll meet a lot of nice consultants. You won't be held accountable for your mistakes. And you'll have a job for life.

Of doers and doodlers

I know four bits of German. The first three of them, in what seems to me to be the right order, are tank, leather trousers and eleven beers please. I learned them on a cricket tour of the British Army of the Rhine.

My fourth bit of German is the useful word Zeitgeist. It means literally the ghost of the time, less literally the spirit of the age. But though I like the word Zeitgeist, I do not like its present manifestation. For I am out of tune with the Zeitgeist.

The Zeitgeist requires us to be driven people. Efficiency is today's watchword. We are to be busy and keen, urged on by achievement, lured by the dangling carrot of success, booting the football of hope towards the goals that we have set for ourselves somewhere on the level playing field of life.

All of which is well and good if that's the way you're made but not everyone is, or at least I'm not, and nor was Bill Vaughan. Bill Vaughan's dead but he used to write newspaper columns, one of which I read in the lavatory this morning and I discovered that Billyboy reckoned to spend, on average, twenty-seven minutes of every working day straightening paper-clips.

And with those few words Bill Vaughan reached out from the grave and up through the plumbing and he seized me. That's the power of literature for you. He told me I was not alone. Here was a man I could do business with. Or rather here was a man I could do anything but business with.

For Bill Vaughan, bless his portable Olivetti, was a waster of time, a procrastinator, a ditherer, and so am I and I'll be damned before I think it a sin.

But there, look there on that word 'waster'. In that word you can sense the grim grey Zeitgeist worming into my consciousness and tinkling the little bell of guilt. Straightening paper-clips, it says in its thin puritan whine, is wasting time.

But it isn't. Oh no, and here, bolstered by Bill, I set my standard in the ground and I shall not be moved. Though I fight till my knees buckle and my body sways, as long as I can stand I shall defend the art of wasting time. I have straightened a thousand paper-clips and I shall not be ashamed. The French call paper-clips trombones, but whatever you call them they are made for straightening.

The Zeitgeist says they are for clipping papers. The Zeitgeist says they are for attaching mission statements to strategic plans. But I see every straightened trombone as a tiny act of rebellion against the zealots of efficiency. And a paper-clip once straightened can never be returned to its former condition. It can be used to scrape under fingernails, to carvc doodles on the sticky patina of my desk, to probe into wads of earwax in a manner that has the busybodies from OSH screaming into their filing cabinets, but never again will it clip papers.

Of course this issue is bigger than paper-clips and Bill and I are not alone. Malcolm Muggeridge, he of the face like an ancient apple and the voice that crackled like canvas, he is of our company. He even called his autobiography *Chronicles of Wasted Time*. When Muggeridge left India after a stint at a university he found a wad of unmarked exam scripts in his bag. And as he steamed slowly towards England he sat in a deckchair at the stern of his ship and rigorously marked each script, writing marginal comments, totting up figures, and then when he was done with it, he tossed it over the side. You can only admire such pointlessness, such spectacular wasting of time.

And Philip Larkin too knew all about wasting time. He called it 'time torn off unused'. And furthermore it was Larkin who observed that it matters little what you do with time for 'however you use it, it goes'.

And I am happiest letting it trickle through my fingers. I love nothing better than to muse, to woolgather, to find an old newspaper in a drawer when looking for something else and to spend half a morning reading it, to stare out of windows, to throw sticks for dogs, to paddle in the shallows of thought. The world is various, and wasting time is simply to float in its variety, to accept it rather than to try to affect it.

In Evelyn Waugh's *Decline and Fall* there's a mad architect – anyone for pleonasm? – called Otto Silenus who reckons that people should be divided not by sex but by disposition. There are, he says, dynamic people and static people. I would call them doers and doodlers, and of the two types I would like to think I know who are the happier. Eleven beers please.

Fat fight

Most diets are mad and sad.

I have never been on a diet but now two of my male friends are. One has had something wrong with his heart and is forbidden all food except celery. Animal fats are a particular no-no. I have never quite understood this business about animal fats in that they don't seem to do animals much harm, but I probably shouldn't question medical science.

Anyway, because friend 1 had the heart problem, friend two, who is roughly the same age, went scuttling to his doctor. The doctor looked him over, listened to bits of him, palpated other bits, fired x-rays through the remaining bits and pronounced him fit, well, radiant but a stone overweight. The stone had to go.

And now friend two's a bore. He refuses invitations to parties. He spends his lunchtimes with tweezers picking the calories from his sandwiches. Frying bacon sends him squealing from the kitchen like a piglet. He looks miserable and no thinner. And that, in my experience, is the truth of diets: people on them have little fun.

Of course it is mainly women who diet and they don't diet for reasons of health. They diet in order to become attractive people. But the diet makes them irritable and their failure to stick to it makes them miserable. Irritability and misery make them unattractive people. I don't pretend to understand.

Everybody seemed to love the Two Fat Ladies. What they liked about them was that they were fat. What they liked even more about them was that they were happy. And what they liked most of all was that they were themselves. Individuality is sexy. I never saw the two fatsos on television but I did read one of their recipes. It consisted mainly of cream and butter and they strongly recommended that it should be served with cream. I admired it hugely. But what I admired even more was their disdain for received wisdom.

I gather that one of the Two Fat Ladies is now dead but I doubt if she's too worried about it. And I have no doubt that the other one is still up to her gills in the trough.

Diets don't just make people miserable. They also presume people are stupid. When I first saw a book called, if I recall, *The Hip and Thigh Diet*, I thought it was a joke. Do certain foods fatten certain parts? Is there a breast diet or a wrist diet or an eyelid diet? For all I know there may be, but certainly there's a liver-cleansing diet. It has made the author millions. Every day I must walk all unknowing past a hundred people whose livers are gleaming like dewdrops in the sun. I hope they feel better for it. I am actually writing a diet book of my own at present. It's called *Scrub That Pancreas*. Publishers are queuing for the rights.

Every women's magazine features a new diet. Again I do not understand. If the new diet is there because the old one didn't work, what evidence is there that the new one will? There is none, but that doesn't seem to matter. Hope springs eternal in the chubby buttock.

Diets are so varied that you can choose one that pleases. This seems even more bizarre. Years ago and in a foreign country, I taught with a spectacularly vain man who kept a comb and mirror in a cupboard in his classroom. When once I caught him dolling himself up between lessons his face went the colour of a bruise.

Nevertheless this man was a trencherman of the first order, and particularly fond of fine wine and tender meats. When someone suggested falsely that his trousers were looking a little tight he went in search of a diet. It took him only a few hours to discover the steak and red wine diet. He stuck to it rigidly, lost no weight but believed that he had. Dieting, it seems, is part self-hatred and part self-love. And all the rest's delusion.

And I must profess a fondness for big people. The television ads that imply that the large are all sad don't tally with my experience. An old friend of mine called John was the best company one could hope for. His mind was whetted, his wit infectious and he was as fat as a barrel of dripping. He liked being fat and did all that he could to get fatter. His doctor charged him by the acre.

John's mother worried about her son's fat and on his twenty-eighth birthday she sent him a kitset rowing machine. I was there when it arrived. John asked me what it was. I told him. He sent it back to the manufacturer to be fitted with an ashtray.

Then John met a woman. She came from California. Worse still, she was a lawyer. In defiance of all reason John fell in love with her. She rewarded him by putting him on a diet. He drinks mineral water now and goes to the gym. Or at least, that is what my friends tell me. John, the slim and miserable sod, no longer answers my letters.

Einstein's bus

According to Einstein, time can travel at different speeds. I think that Einstein must have frequented bus-stops, for nowhere in the universe does time travel more slowly than when waiting for a bus. Bus-stops are built in the gap between tick and tock.

But you can learn a lot from bus-stops. At the bus-stop on Norwich Quay I have learned that there is a group called the West Lyttelton Thugs. They have carved their title into the bus-stop bench. I have also learned that James Burwood is a victim of phonetic language teaching. 'James Burwood was hear 1999,' wrote James. Or I presume James wrote it. It is of course possible that one of the West Side Thugs wrote it so as to get James into trouble. Perhaps James beat one of them in a spelling test.

But whoever was hear I know how they felt. Waiting for a bus is as frustrating as impotence. There's nothing to do but hope that the bus might come. James was hear in 1999 but it doesn't say how much of 1999 he was hear for. It is raining and it is cold and I feel as if I have been hear for about a yere.

Only the graffiti entertains me. 'Welcome to Lyttleton,' says the wall of the shelter, 'watch out for inbreeding.' I am watching out, but all I can see is the wind and the rain and the grey-brown sea, the rusting trawlers, the blackly shining street and one old woman limping through the puddles. Every other Lytteltonian is wisely at home, drinking gin by the heated indoor gene-pool.

It's the Queen's birthday. By now she will have opened her presents – oooh look, an eviction notice. So thoughtful, Charles, but really, I couldn't possibly – and the party games will have begun. Right at this moment they may be pinning the tail on the fiancee. Ever the loyal subject I hold my own party game. I spy with my little eye something beginning with 'n'. No bus.

I would welcome any sign of life. Where are the West Side boys when I could use a bit of thuggery? Whear is James Burwood? Not hear, just as I would prefer not to be. I would rather be at home but, as I say, you learn a lot from bus-stops. I am learning that next time I go to town for a night out I should not take my car. For now I have to go back to town to fetch it in the bus that doesn't come. The rain drums on the shelter and drips darkly down the metal. The timetable behind its perspex cover is obscured by condensation. The future is unreadable.

I approve of public transport. It makes such sense. Put fifty people in a bus and leave fifty cars at home. Less petrol, less smog, less noise, and far fewer cars to get in the way of my car. For though a bus is more worthy, I shall keep to my car. People throughout history have dreamed of a vehicle that takes you wherever you want to go while you sit down. They called it a Turkish carpet. We call it a car and we like it. But mine is in town. Someone should invent a car that comes when you whistle.

A bus-stop may have made a physicist of Einstein, but of most of us it makes a philosopher. For what is life if it isn't waiting for a bus that doesn't come? Shakespeare could have written a play about it. Beckett probably did. My life centres on an absent bus. It is the transport of delight which hasn't arrived, the prayer unanswered, the dream not yet made diesel. 'O Big Red, I am gathered here together in the presence of weather and the absence of car. Look down, I beseech thee, on this thy wet servant. O Big Red, where are you?' And suddenly the bus arrives. The sense of impotence evaporates.

The bus's windows are misted, its driver friendly, its seats barren of people. The engine strains, the bus accelerates and time accelerates with it. On the wall a red hammer. 'In emergency remove hammer to smash glass.' All emergency notices make me want an emergency.

The bus trawls through the suburbs collecting people who climb aboard and shake themselves like dogs. At Cathedral Square the rubber doors release me back into the rain, but I am purposeful now, in command of time and destiny, hurrying to where I ditched my car. As I turn into Hereford Street I am seized by the fear that the car will have gone. But there it is, mute and stationary with the brute patience of a mere thing. Time means nothing to a car. For most of its life it merely waits. But for me now it is my wish fulfilled, my independence restored, the best possible present on the Queen's birthday and there in the sodden street I want to hug it like a long-lost sister.

Prizing advice

Some while ago I took up golf and I wrote, 'Nothing in life has so confirmed my fear that I have reached middle age.' I apologise for quoting myself here but, more importantly, I apologise for being wrong. For five minutes ago a phone call proved me wrong. It seems that I am not in middle age; I am in old age. In shuffling slippers I have rounded the final corner in the great race and am tottering towards the tape before an empty grandstand. The timekeeper yawns, glances at his watch and cocks his finger above the button that says stop. I am as old and slow and wrinkled as a tortoise. I have a spine like a stick of chalk. I mumble through gums, suck eggs and snooze. Soon I shall snap like a water biscuit.

I know all this because the man who telephoned me, you see, was a school principal. Would I, he asked, care to address his school prize-giving?

I have seen school prize-givings. In thirty-something years in schools, a dozen of them spent learning little and twenty of them teaching less, I have seen them all. I have heard a swag of boring bishops. I have heard a herd of entrepreneurs, smug with suits and wise with wallets, returning to the scene of the crimes of childhood and telling lies. I have heard famous sportspeople mumble platitudes about passion and dedication and hard work paying off, and the need for that horror of horrors, goal-setting. I have heard the fat-chested cock of immodesty crow loud and long about yesterday. I have sat through a man telling 600 children that at the age of fifteen he suddenly developed an unquenchable fascination with parrots, the breeding and showing thereof, and he urged the children to do likewise. I have endured military men encrusted with medals for having sent younger men to their death, and I have heard them say that life is a battle and that it pays to have God on your side and a couple of tanks. I have heard them all and I have even, God help me, smiled politely at their jokes.

The children haven't. The children have yawned, fidgeted, stirred, scratched themselves, fingered the cigarettes in their pockets, eyed the exits manned by teachers with folded arms and have switched their brains into neutral and their ears into stops. And now they will yawn, fidget, stir, scratch, finger, eye and switch in front of me. And they are wise.

For to what does the mind of a crusty oldster turn when invited to address children? As inevitably as a weathervane turns to the wind, it turns to advice. And in no field of human endeavour has so much air been vibrated to so little purpose as in the giving of advice. Advice is a refugee; everyone wishes to pass it on but no one wishes to receive it.

And is the advice of the old worth listening to? Are parrots, the breeding and showing thereof, the key to life? Do God and tanks make good allies? Is it wise to set goals? I do not think so. Nor do I think that in the years I have lived I have learned very much of value to pass on. I remain the ignorant fool I always was. I may walk more slowly and suffer worse hangovers, but I continue to make the errors I made as a child. I have just got better at hiding them. Character is destiny, said Novalis and I am with him. It's what happens to happen, said Larkin and I am with him.

And there, in those last two sentences, you have it. Over the years I have collected a few nuggets of other people's wisdom. I have not surveyed the map of my experience and seen the world afresh. I have just stumbled from hap to mishap, read a few books on the way and picked up some pretty phrases like a bright-eyed, dull-brained magpie.

But let us suppose otherwise. Let us suppose for the moment that I had the wisdom of the ages and the wit of David Lange. Would it profit the world that I went to the prize-giving, reared to my feet to insincere applause and cast my wisdom about me like grain to fall where it will, some of it lodging perhaps in the heads of a few of the little darlings dragooned into sitting in patient rows before me, and, having lodged, sprouting into a beacon that will guide them through the dark alleys of their lives to come? No, it would not, for three simple reasons: one is that grains cannot sprout into beacons, the second is that the children would not be listening and the third is that nobody acts on advice.

I know so. For in the twenty years of teaching I have dispensed tons of the stuff. I have run two boarding houses and sprayed advice about me like a fountain. None of it did any good. The most salutary experience occurred when a boy in Canada came to talk to me after the others had gone to bed. He brought with him a toothbrush. We chatted about the toothbrush, then he told me that his mother had multiple sclerosis. He told me that she was deteriorating. He told me that he was afraid that she would die. He cried. And I could think of nothing to say. When he had said what he had to say he left.

In the morning I sought out a colleague whose wisdom I valued. I told him what had happened. I told him how hopeless I had felt, how I'd found nothing to say, no advice to give.

The wise man told me that, on the contrary, I had done the best thing. I had listened and my silence was the best advice that I could give. And he was right, of course. And now that I think of that story I realise that, if nothing else, I have written my prize-giving speech.

The Fatuous Greetings Company

As you will be aware, it is no easy job to affect the way people greet each other and when we founded our organisation we warned shareholders that they could expect to see little in the way of dividends from The Fatuous Greetings Co. in the first two decades of our existence.

I am delighted to report, however, that success has come more quickly than we dared to expect.

America, of course, is our original base where we are recognised as market leaders. Thus we felt that it would be a good idea to enter the New Zealand inter-personal greetings industry at the same time as the American fast food chains some fifteen years ago. We began our campaign modestly with a single phrase, on the theory that if we focused on market penetration from the outset then every subsequent innovation would be easier to effect. The phrase we chose was 'Have a nice day'. It is a proven winner.

Its combination of vacuousness and apparent bonhomie made it a immediate success in the American market some fifty years ago and it has since swept through much of the English-speaking world. We had some fears that the more rugged and independent New Zealand market would resist its introduction, but our fears prove unfounded. After initial ridicule – for which we had budgeted – the phrase has become a stock item in New Zealand commercial idiom and our market research suggests that it has, as hoped, now taken its place in everyday social discourse, often in the variant form of 'Have a nice one'.

Because of the 'Have a nice day' success we have been able to implement the next stages of our strategic plan several years ahead of schedule.

Since 'Have a nice day' is a valediction or farewell flourish, our next mission was to popularise a 'front-ender', a phrase that can be employed early in a conversation. We introduced 'How has your day been?' in early 1996. It began slowly but in the last 12 months has risen hugely in common usage (see fig. 3). Vivien Bishop, one of our field operatives, cites the recent example of a dental receptionist who enquired 'How has your day been so far?' of a client at 8.30 in the morning. We believe shareholders will be as excited as we are to see that the phrase is already being used without regard to its meaning. It took 'How do you do?' several centuries to achieve the divorce between meaning and usage that we have achieved in a mere few years.

Now we are galloping ahead. Our recent introduction of 'Have you got a big weekend planned?' has already shown promise in the retail sector. We have also grown the farewell market by the introduction of 'Take care' which has found ready acceptance in the middle-aged consumer bracket. Its stronger variant, 'Take care out there', also seems to be taking root. We ascribe the success of these phrases to the increased perception among the older generation that the world has become hostile. We confidently predict strong growth in this sector.

At the same time our infiltration policy has been two-pronged. A subsidiary arm of The Fatuous Greetings Co. has focused on the youth market and a glance at its yield curve (fig. 10) will confirm that its growth has far exceeded expectations. The biggest winners here have been monosyllabic. Both 'yo' and 'bro' have been runaway successes and are now acknowledged brand leaders in the youth greetings industry. The most remarkable innovation, however, and one that has surprised even us, is the renewed popularity of the greeting 'man', a line that we discontinued in 1973.

The youth market has been supported with an intensive merchandising campaign. Much of our success is certainly owed to the material inducements of baseball caps and distinctively baggy trousers. In addition to this, however, and this is where we believe we stand apart from our competitors, we have innovated a form of physical merchandising, what we have dubbed manner-ism. Our first venture in this field of greetings was the hand slap known as 'the high five'. It proved so popular among the young that we have since introduced the double handshake, involving the shoulder-high overlocking thumb grip followed by the more conventional joining of hands, accompanied of course by any combination of our monosyllablic youth greetings.

We are pleased, therefore, to announce a dividend to our investors well ahead of schedule and are confident of far greater yields in the years to come.

The compiler of this company report acknowledges his debt to Francis Wheen.

Snakehitch

In a poem called 'Snake', D.H. Lawrence tells how, in the heat of the day, he went to a water trough to drink and found a snake there before him. The snake was venomous and Lawrence had to wait in line. I have always liked the poem, partly for the description of the slack-bellied snake and the precise way it sips at the water trough, but more for the way the poem ends.

Last night it was raining. I was driving up the motorway towards the Lyttelton tunnel having spent the evening playing pool in a garage and sipping at good beer, drinking it slowly like whisky, making the bottle last, because I would be driving home. My companions were a taxi driver who played flamboyantly and a slack-bellied Internet entrepreneur who was surprisingly diffident and warm of heart and who owned the pool table and the garage. I played lucky pool, beat them both several times and then we sat on plastic chairs to smoke and talk about God and literacy and race. It was a fine evening.

Beside the motorway a youth was hitching. He should not have been. The car ahead of me slowed. When the youth ran towards it the car drove away, the kids in the back seat leaning out of the window in the rain to laugh at the hitchhiker. He raised fingers to them.

Because I did not learn to drive a car until I was twenty-eight, and because I travelled many thousands of miles by thumb, I always pick up hitchhikers unless their appearance scares me. I stopped. The youth was drenched and when he climbed into the front seat I could smell the beer on him. I asked him where he was going. Akaroa, I thought he said.

I was going only as far as Lyttelton. Akaroa was an hour of hilly backroads beyond. In such weather and at such a time of night the youth stood little chance of getting a lift. I told him so. He did not reply. I looked across and his eyes were closed.

I nudged him awake and said it all again.

'I've got all night,' he said. 'It's taken all day to get out of Hamilton.'

'Hamilton?'

'Got to get to Tokoroa. I live in Tokoroa,' he said, as if explaining to someone stupid. His eyes started to close again.

I was unsure what to do.

'You know you're in Christchurch, don't you?'

'Yeah,' he said, but he didn't.

I kept him talking through the tunnel. I did not want him falling asleep in the car. I felt discomfited, not by his peaceable drunkenness but by his unreason. I also knew that I should give him a bed for the night, breakfast in the bright morning and then send him on his way. But I didn't want to. I didn't want the inconvenience.

He said he was a student. Exams were in a fortnight. I asked him if he was running away from something but the question got no answer. I repeated that I was going only as far as Lyttelton where I lived. He said that was fine but I don't believe he heard me. My words were noise.

We came out of the tunnel and turned a corner and I stopped the car. He was fast asleep again. I nudged him and he asked me if we were in Tokoroa. I told him we were in Lyttelton and this was as far as I could take him. He fumbled a bit for the door catch and then got out and walked down the street. This side of the hills it was not raining but below the streetlights the wind of midnight billowed his shirt of red check. I watched him down the road. For a drunk he walked remarkably straight.

I drove home, greeted the dogs, checked for telephone messages and found I had none, then put my jacket back on, got back into the car and drove round Lyttelton to look for the youth and offer him a bed for the night. The bars had almost all closed. I couldn't find him. I wondered what he would be doing, whether he was curled in a garage or had found a lift further into confusion. I knew I had failed him. My selfishness had failed him and I felt guilt.

This morning the guilt is only a niggle. By tomorrow it will have gone.

At the end of the poem Lawrence threw a log at the snake. Its tail writhed and it was gone and Lawrence was left with regret. He knew he had let himself down, had betrayed some sense of fitness, rightness.

'And I have something to expiate,' wrote Lawrence, 'a pettiness.'

On noticing the shags

It is a law of life, or at least it is a law of my life, that you don't notice something until someone draws your attention to it. And as soon as they do draw your attention to it, you can't stop noticing it. For example, if someone says that it's been a good year for the yellow-bellied shag, I say 'What?'

'The yellow-bellied shag,' they say. 'Look.'

I look and what do I see but shags in all directions, diving and swooping on flowers and fish, their yellow bellies gleaming in the sun.

'Oh, of course, the yellow-bellied shag,' I say. 'I thought you said Macquarie Island shag', but all the time I am marvelling at how I missed all those shags – though at my age that is not an uncommon thought. But now I see shags everywhere, their bellies as yellow as butter.

But the converse of the shag theory is also true – if you pay no attention to something it isn't there. It is the ostrich theory. Ostriches famously hide by sinking their heads into sand. If they can't see the enemy, the enemy doesn't exist.

Ostriches have taken a lot of stick for this manoeuvre – not least from their enemies, and not always pleasantly – but in fact ostriches are wise birds. More often than not, if you hide from something it does go away. If, for example, you don't turn on the news the government disappears. And the same seems to be true of tonsils.

Last year my tonsils mutinied. Immediately I became a tonsil bore and discovered that everyone, but everyone, had a tonsil story that had previously lain buried beneath my lack of interest. It seemed that the whole world pulsed with tonsils.

My tonsils proved instructive. After skirmishing for a few weeks they went properly to war. They hurled infections at me. I lobbed penicillin back, but the infections skulked like Chechen rebels in the rugged crevices of Tonsilland, waited for the antibiotic cloud to pass, then rose again revitalised to wage the war afresh.

Eventually they sent me to hospital where the nurses wheeled out the serious artillery. They injected stuff into me. They dripped stuff into me. The infections came out with their hands up like germs in a toilet cleaner ad. I left the hospital with a song in my heart and youth in my throat.

But the hospital knew more about tonsils than I. They told me that once a tonsil had turned treacherous, it could never be trusted to be a loyal citizen again. It might doff its cap as the monarch passed, but all the while it would be fingering the knife in its belt and muttering words of treason.

'We have scotched the snake,' said the doctors, 'not killed it. Have those tonsils out and be done with it.'

I have never undergone surgery. I would prefer not to undergo surgery but I accepted.

Well, soon afterwards the hospital sent me a nice letter. It said that the condition of my tonsils earned me fifty points. It was a bit like air-miles. In the present state of waiting lists fifty points entitled me to have my operation at no time in the foreseeable future. If, however, my condition improved and I no longer needed the operation I couldn't have, would I be kind enough to let them know so that they could slot someone else into my place in the list to wait for it.

'Sure,' I said and promptly did an ostrich. It worked. I forgot about my tonsils and my tonsils forgot about me. Effectively they ceased to exist.

That was six healthy months ago. Last week the hospital rang me in exultant form. They had got more money. They could take my tonsils out whenever I wished. I said I didn't wish. God, I said, had joined me and my tonsils together and let no man put us asunder. Besides, I said, they didn't hurt any more.

'Well done,' said the hospital, 'bravo', and we parted on terms of mutual praise. I said they were a nice hospital and they said I was a clever little tonsil conqueror.

That night I dreamt that my tonsils hurt. The next morning they did. The morning after that they hurt some more. I rang the hospital.

'You know that tonsil business,' I said.

'We were waiting for you to call,' they said. In the background I caught the sound of scalpels being sharpened.

I am sure that if the hospital hadn't reminded me of them my tonsils would have behaved. The mind, it seems, has a mind of its own. And now I sit at my desk, looking out of the window, dreading the pain of a tonsillectomy and barely noticing the swooping and chortling of a flock of yellow-bellied shags.

Poker man

The other day I was asked to name my hero. I said I knew who he was, but I couldn't name him.

Hero worship is close cousin to envy. In many cases our heroes are our heroes because they have done what we would like to do. If Todd Blackadder is our hero it is because we aspire to lead the All Blacks. If Shakespeare is our hero it is because we want to be read.

That we can rarely match the feats of our heroes perhaps explains why we are hard on them, although the claim that New Zealand is especially hard on heroes does not bear scrutiny. It was, for example, a British pornographic newspaper which exposed Mark Todd rather than a New Zealand one. Smashing idols has been a popular pastime the world over since the first ape stood erect.

With my own hero I spent a night on a foreign railway station some twenty years ago, but to make sense of the story I need to go back.

The only career decision I ever made was not to be a teacher. In the end I taught for twenty years and loved it. But when one day in the bar at university, shortly before I was due to venture out into the wide world armed with an impressive overdraft and an unimpressive degree, a friend called Dave drew my attention to a personal ad in the paper, saying 'English graduates wanted to teach English in Spain', I snorted.

In emphatic terms I told Dave that I spoke no Spanish, I had no desire to go to Spain and under no circumstances would I ever teach. And then I bought him a beer for being thoughtful.

Two weeks later I received a letter inviting me to interview for the job. Dave had not only applied on my behalf, he had even snipped my face from a rugby team photo to accompany the application. I would not have gone to the interview but it was in London where I wanted to attend a party and the interview offered to pay expenses. I hitched there and claimed the train fare.

The interviewer was a scrawny bearded man. Within two minutes he had told me he played first five for the Spanish national team. Within five minutes he and I were passing a paperweight between us. Within ten minutes he had convinced me that I would play halfback for Spain and I had accepted the job. We didn't discuss teaching at all.

Some weeks later, after forty-eight hours of sleepless travel, I arrived at Zaragoza railway station. I rang the number on my letter of appointment. I got an angry monolingual Spaniard. I tried again. The same Spaniard, only angrier. I went to the station bar, drank a thoughtful beer, then rang the number once more. The phone was off the hook. It was 11 o'clock at night. It was only then that I realised that the whole thing was a hoax. No job existed. Dave had brilliantly marooned me in Spain with no job, no money, no return ticket, no Spanish beyond yes, no and beer and, as I was rapidly discovering, no spine. On Zaragoza railway station I sat down and wept.

And it was then on that station forecourt, deserted but for drunks sheltering from the cold, that my hero entered on cue, tapping an umbrella as he walked. He was English, sixty-five years old and dressed in a pepper and salt suit. By profession he played poker. Whenever he won a wad of money he went hitchhiking round Europe. He commandeered lifts with his umbrella and went where the whim took him. In his little holdall he carried spare underwear, a clean shirt and a metal detector. He liked to hunt for Roman coins he said, but had found very few. I told him my tale. He laughed. And he made me laugh. We talked till two in the morning then slept side by side on the bench.

The cafeteria opened at six. The old man bought me an omelette and a coffee with brandy in it, then left. As I type this I can see him now, his umbrella tapping on the steps leading out of the station, and beyond him dawn rising over a country I didn't know.

Why my hero? For his disdain of conventional wisdom, his bloody-minded independence, his courage, his light-heartedness, his grace under pressure, but above all for the way he made me feel that all things were possible. He gave me strength. Two decades later he still does. I think that's what a hero should do.

The job, by the way, did exist. The school had changed its phone number.

The long slide to paradise

Like most good things, skiing costs a lot and serves no purpose. If you believe in evolution then skiing suggests it's come to an end. Man no longer has to fight to survive. At the weekend he can afford time off from hunting and child-rearing to don hundreds of dollars' worth of clothes, rent thousands of dollars' worth of equipment, and ride millions of dollars-worth of ski-lift up the side of a mountain in order to slide down it.

But if you don't believe in evolution, if you believe that God made man in his own image, then one glance at the skifield and you get doubts. If these people dressed in puffer-fish jackets and wigwam hats are baby godlings then it suggests nasty things about the manufacturer of the universe, suggests indeed that earth is probably a cosmic joke, which of course it is. And skiing is part of the fun.

When I was a kid at school we made ice-slides by pouring water on the playground. They worked best in winter. Once they had frozen we ran at the ice, hit it at speed and slid with feet a shoulder's width apart and arms spread like wings, whooping and squealing all the way to the end of the ice. Then we fell over. But the five-second slide was a wonder. It was cheating the natural order of things; it was movement without effort. We felt like gods, like free-wheeling kings of locomotion, the albatrosses of solid earth, untameable lords of creation. Ice-sliding was the childhood equivalent of gin.

The other joy of ice-slides was that they were illegal. Teachers with gloves and moustaches banned them. Ice-sliding, said the teachers, was dangerous. We could break bones. What the teachers meant was that if they tried it, they would break bones. Their osteoporotic hips would shatter like chalk. We never broke bones. We skinned knees and banged heads and funny-boned elbows into numb agony but we were fine. We were the flexible gods. We had rubber bones, the bones of young chickens. The teachers banned the ice-slides for the same reason adults ban all children's activities – envy.

Adults like all children's games. Adults at parties drink gin, talk politics and think sex, but they would rather play sardines. In their hearts adults prefer *Hairy Maclary* to *Anna Karenina*. They prefer *The Simpsons* to the news. But guilt makes them want to attain some mythical status called adulthood. Adulthood equals seriousness. It probably stems from having money.

Skiing, then, is the perfect adult pastime. It reverts to childhood but it appears serious because it costs a lot. The expense validates the exercise. It also validates the Pajero. One annual trip up the ski-road justifies the rest of the year puttering from home to mall to school in a vehicle built of testosterone.

Because skiing is just ice-sliding made expensive, it is best done by children. Infants use skis as a dolphin uses flippers. Toss a new-born child onto a ski slope and it will start doing parallel turns. Toss a fully fledged adult onto a ski slope and it turns into a child who can't stand up. Adults use skis as a dolphin uses a can-opener.

Just as ski slopes come in degrees of difficulty, so skiers come in levels of incompetence. The level not to be at is adult-beginner level. Adults cherish dignity which they achieve by relinquishing all activities that look undignified. Dancing is one such activity. So is sex. So, in excelsis, is learning to ski.

For the adult beginner, putting one ski on is a breeze. Putting the second on is a farce. Like any farce it involves a lot of falling over. Unlike a farce it involves falling over in full view of thousands of brightly coloured children who ski past at a speed that resembles a noise.

To learn to stand up and slide, adults hire an instructor who doesn't speak English. Instructors who do speak English are working in Austria. This is part of a global plan to make ski lessons incomprehensible. The longer you remain at the toddler stage the more lessons you have to pay for.

Nevertheless the beginner eventually masters the snowplough. This means grinding down the bottom bit of the learner slope at a speed that resembles reverse. The correct physical posture for this exercise is that of a man squatting over an foreign lavatory. The correct facial expression is terror.

But once the terror leaves, the pleasure comes. The pleasure of sliding down slopes which the grooming machine has turned into alpine streets. The pleasure of speed, of innocent danger, of whooping to the frosted air, of trailing clouds of glory, of falling down and laughing and getting up and going again, of letting go of adulthood to snatch at the tantalising tail of freedom, fun and folly. Like life itself it is pointless, expensive, downhill and glorious. Could you ask for more?

Sprung

If neglect could kill a garden, we would long since have been singing hymns over mine and saying what a good chap it was really despite that gruff exterior. But neglect doesn't kill a garden. It just encourages it. And now my garden's got spring.

Spring springs. Was anything ever better named than spring? I can think only of a boy I taught called S. Melling. He did.

But like all things that spring – leopards, debt-collectors, the handles of rakes when you tread on the tines – spring packs a sleeveful of surprise. I never see it coming. One moment the garden's a wet dump of dogbones, and the next it's got blossom sprouting impossibly from fruit trees that looked dead. Blossom's a con. It's just a tree tarting itself up to get pollinated, but it moves the bees to groping and me to sentimentality.

I find television moving too. Most often I move out of the room. But I recall a televised interview with the writer Dennis Potter. He was dying of innumerable complaints about which he didn't complain. Psoriasis had racked him all his life. Cancer was eating him. During the interview he swigged morphine from a hip-flask. He knew he had seen his last spring. And he spoke of the blossom of that spring and he said, and I quote, it was 'the blossomest blossom' of his life. The blossomest blossom is a phrase to cuddle and clutch, to sniff and cradle. That's what I mean by sentimentality. Spring does strange things.

This morning the sun thunders into this house like a blessing, reminding me of the ancient immutable truth that my windows are filthy. I know how to fix filthy windows. But right now I don't want to move house.

Spring is caprice. e e cummings called it 'a perhaps hand'. Fate toys with it. By the time you read this, rain may be lashing the roof and spanking the windows, but it won't matter. In a few fine days the earth has made a promise and has stirred my urban blood. It's put platform soles on my soul. I share in the land's surprise and am in awful danger of writing verse. If you catch any rhyme popping into this prose, please pass me the gun and summon the wise woman with the winding sheet and bury me beneath the daffodillies where the soft wind blows.

Lambs dot the fields. Lambs are chops on the hoof, but spring has infected those hooves. The lambs make odd little lunatic leaps of apparent happiness. It's called gambolling but the odds are stacked against them. The long shadow of the freezing works stands on the far side of summer. Nevertheless the lambs leap in dumb joy, and so do I. Though this morning I stopped leaping to listen to a blackbird. Spring is dangerous for a chap. But I don't think anyone saw me.

The signs of spring are everywhere. Spring is forgetting the tumble drier and pinning clothes to the line with plastic pegs made brittle by a winter of frosts. I pegged this morning for the first time in two months and three pegs broke. Through my kitchen window now I can see a shirt steaming.

Throughout the winter smokers have hunched outside office blocks, presenting as little as possible to the air's teeth, and blowing the smoke at their boots. Now they lounge, stretch, sprawl on warm concrete steps, turn their faces to the sun and blow smoke at it in puffs of hope. Beneath them the earth breathes out and expands and stirs like a long giant.

Stop it. Next thing I know I'll be sprouting a bad beard and sacrificing something. But fertility rites seem right this morning. The Green Goddess stalks the soil. With a heigh and a ho and a heigh nonny no.

No.

People will spoil the spring. The wrong people will pull on shorts and their Christmas-turkey thighs will make the universe pause, will make it wonder if spring is an error and winter the way to stay. But the sun has promised now and it cannot go back on its word. The dogs are moulting. Spring is a bedful of dog hair and a boost to the bones.

Spring has slid into every house in this street and every red-blooded man has felt the pulse of new life and been touched by the primitive urge to mow his lawn. The air this morning is sweet with the smell of two-stroke. And I'm going out with the dogs to sniff it. Now.

This is terribly emotional

Last week was National Poetry Week or Day or something, but whatever it was the wise went into hiding. Only now that it's over are the wise emerging from their underground shelters, blinking at the sunlight and still looking nervously around in case some character in a home-knitted jersey with stains should shamble up to them and fix them with his glittering eye and start reading from a slim volume.

At university I learned all about these amateur poetry johnnies. They used to lurk in bars, always in sensitive jerseys, some even polo-necked, their shaking pianist's fingers clutching half-pints of mild beer from which they never drank. The jerseys and the untouched beer should have been warning enough but these people were cunning.

They would take an intense interest in that most permanently interesting of subjects, me. I would say something and they would lean across the table and say 'Oh really', and gaze at me with spaniel eyes, 'Oh really, that's terribly interesting', which of course it was because I had said it. And as I was young and easy under the apple bough, I fell for their flattery like any honest housewife for a brush salesman.

The jersey-wearing poets probably had a little manual for snaring suckers like me, a manual explaining just how to sit in bars looking empathetic, how to draw me in to spit out all the butt ends of my days and ways, in short, how to soften me up before moving in for the kill. And because I could not discern the difference between interest in me – which was admirable – and feigned interest in me – which was inconceivable – I fell for it every time.

Oh there was warning enough, but I was blind to the signs. For a while all would go swimmingly. I would deliver a Bennett monologue eloquent with grief, surrendering my heart of anger to the stranger, and punctuated only by the jersey's tuts and moans of sympathy, but then the conversation would take a subtle and ominous turn. The 'How you've suffered, my dear', which was both gratifying and bang on, would become 'My dear, how we've suffered', which was neither. At that point I should, of course, have reared to my feet, swallowed the half-pint of mild in a single gulp, tossed the glass over my shoulder, proclaimed that no coward soul was mine and stalked imperious and alone into the great night of self-pity. But I never did.

Soon afterwards the shutters would fall on the bar like a prison door slamming with me on the wrong side of it, and I would be out on the street with the jersey, and somehow, imperceptibly, the conversation would turn on its head. Instead of speaking I would find myself listening, an activity which is rarely wise and never pleasant, and then inevitably there came the fateful invitation. The jersey's rooms were just around the corner and would I, perhaps, care to round off the evening with a little drink? In the hope of scotch I would follow. The consequences were unspeakable and the scotch always, but always, turned out to be cocoa.

But worse, far worse, than the cocoa was the poetry. How did I never see it coming? Oh beat at this pate that let this folly in and my poor judgment out, but soon I would be sunk in an armchair and the jersey would be sunk in another and he – it was nearly always he, though once or twice and every bit as horribly it wasn't – would reach for a cloth-bound notebook and with an 'I thought perhaps you might like…' he would open it and cough and start to read and I would be a possum in the headlights.

The poetry was ghastly. It was all love and death and skeletal trees and mossy thighs and sagging fenceposts, but worse even than the poetry was the voice. You know the poetry reading voice, the this-is-terribly-emotional voice, all hushed and reverential. You can still hear it sometimes on the radio. It is the voice of undressing for non-sexual purposes, the voice of the guidance counsellor after a yoga session, bowel-twisting, precious, breathy, earnest and wrong. It turns my spine to chicken skin.

There would be nothing I could do. The poet chap would have me sprawling on a pin. When finally I escaped after what seemed like years I would run through the night, drawing lungfuls of air and shouting my horror to the skies, and when finally I regained my rooms I would collapse with relief on my bed. Beside the bed a dusty table. On the table a cloth-bound notebook. Inside the notebook, well, how do you take your cocoa?

Too many eggs

I have long maintained that cooked food comes in only two types: recognisable and unrecognisable. Recognisable food looks like what it started as. Examples include steak, sausages and goats' heads. All recognisable food is best fried, of course, except for goats' heads, which should be boiled slowly with garlic, bay leaves and balsamic vinegar and then thrown away.

A friend who made the strange decision to woo a Spanish woman was once fed goat's head by his prospective in-laws. Apparently the best part of a goat's head is the gums. The only way to get at the gums is to gnaw. My friend is not a squeamish man – he is Scottish and he likes football – but he confessed to finding it a trial to watch, and hear, his fiancée clashing teeth with a goat. It took, he said, the bloom from romance.

Anyway, because I cook for myself my diet consists entirely of recognisable food. It is only when I eat out that I graze on unrecognisable food, which is defined as stuff cooked by other people in which the ingredients are not immediately evident. Examples of unrecognisable food are cake, hollandaise sauce and everything Indian.

All of which serves only to introduce my egg problem. I have too many eggs. Spring has triggered some biological alarm clock in my chickens' tiny minds, and their ovary ducts are working like the plastic gun which I was given for Christmas when I was six and which fired ping-pong balls at relatives with a gratifying velocity. (Of course, it was the ping-pong balls rather than the relatives which showed the velocity, although when my only aunt copped a beauty in the back of the neck she moved with a swiftness that a glance at her ankles would have suggested was improbable.)

My eggs are splendid things, as dense as a parcel of protons, and I have cooked them in as many ways as I know how, but even I have tired of fried eggs. And although I have given away as many eggs as I can to both my friends I am still embarrassed by a superfluity.

The woman who knows suggested I cook quiche. I realise, of course, that real men don't eat quiche but I love it, and I don't care if it wreaks havoc on my wrists.

The woman who knows assured me quiche was easy. But it requires pastry. I have never done pastry. And when I wrenched Delia Smith from the library I found that she devoted six pages to pastry. I read them with horror. There was a paragraph called 'pastry psychology' and another called 'pastry perversity'. And, most puzzlingly of all, I learned that good pastry requires cold hands.

Lacking a thermometer, I headed for the supermarket where I found an agreeably cheap chunk of ready-made pastry the colour and consistency of a corpse. When I dropped it on the kitchen bench the thud frightened the dogs.

As a child I had seen my mother rolling pastry. She made it look easy. But my mother never tried to roll pastry with a bottle of Queen Adelaide Regency red. The neck of the bottle proved a satisfactory handle. The base of the bottle didn't. And proper rolling pins don't come with a label bearing an embossed picture of Queen Adelaide. Perhaps they should. My pastry was soon dotted with little reverse pictures of Her Majesty which further rolling distorted into hall-of-mirrors monstrosities. It proved rather enjoyable in a republican sort of way.

Transferring the pastry to the pan that would serve as a quiche dish was the sort of activity that makes me grateful that my kitchen is not rigged with surveillance cameras. The dogs prospered. But eventually and after a fashion all was done, and I prodded the pastry into corners and pricked it and baked it blind as Delia told me I should, and I mixed up a pint of cream and a mound of cheese and a foothill or two from my egg mountain, and I poured the sludge into the half-baked pastry and then sat with a fistful of Queen Adelaide to watch my creation become quiche. And it did so with such success that I dined on it for four days running and the dogs grew plump on the burned bits of crust.

And when, out of gratitude, I tossed the final sliver of quiche to the chickens, they sank their beaks into their thwarted genetic inheritance with every appearance of glee. Unrecognisable cooking? I rest my case.

Horace and I

I am fond of Horace the Roman poet. I doubt if my neighbour is.

My neighbour has the right number of male chromosomes. Horace and I have the wrong number. We lack chromosone 101A. That's the one that lays concrete. We also lack 101B – the one that lays everything else – and 101C – the one that tidies things up.

Apparently, cognitive dissonance is where men are at. We like things orderly. Life is a war against disorder. Horace and I lose that war, but we're not men. My neighbour is. He wages the war, fights dirty and means to win.

Right now, Sunday morning shortly after dawn, that exquisitely tender hour when the light is as fragile as eggshell, the hour which John Steinbeck called the hour of the pearl and which other men call nothing at all because they've never seen it except on the way home from the Pig and Chisel, my neighbour's out there with weapons. He's battling the big enemy and he's summoned the big guns. He's laying concrete.

He is where he wants to be and where evolution says he ought to be. I am not. Four hours ago I was in the Pig and Chisel. Now I want to be and ought to be in bed.

My neighbour is fighting nature, otherwise known as entropy, otherwise known as the force that messes things up. Nature has a plan for us and that plan is chaos. Its foot soldiers abound. They are disguised as children, grass, dogs, dust, everything indeed that isn't a man with chromosomes and a concrete mixer. My neighbour's chromosomes are fizzing with evolutionary gratification. He's fulfilling his destiny, fighting the good fight and happy in a way given only to a man playing with big tools.

My neighbour has blocked the road. That, for a start, is a masterful and manly thing to do. He's done it with a concrete mixing truck like a huge rotating egg which has just inched down the hill in reverse to present itself to a pump. The pump has mated with the back of the truck, and is now sucking concrete into an extension that unfurls like a heron's neck. Concrete spews from the heron's beak and everything makes a gratifyingly manly noise, which is why I'm not in bed.

Laying concrete is one in the eye for nature. Nature is deceptively placid. Nature lets us trample it, poison it, weed it, shape it, throw up on it, play cricket on it, make love on it, imagine making love on it and mow it. Then it exacts revenge.

And that's where Horace got it right. 'Naturam expellas furca,' said Horace when his wife told him to leave his poetry and lay concrete, 'tamen usque recurret.' 'You what?' asked his wife. 'You may expel nature with a pitchfork,' sighed Horace, reaching for the gin, 'but from all sides it will come running back.' 'You what?' asked his wife. 'Where's the tonic?' said Horace.

And he was right. Our idea of order differs from nature's idea of order and nature's idea is bigger. Nature, for example, thinks grass should be a foot tall. We think grass should be an inch tall. We buy tools to prove we are right, hugely expensive things with motors to ruin our Sundays. The grass takes it lying down. Then it starts growing again. We can spend our lives mowing the lawn and we do.

My neighbour hasn't read Horace. My neighbour hasn't read anything. He's been too busy mowing and laying concrete. Laying concrete is mowing made drastic. Right now my neighbour is smoothing his lawn into permanent submission. He is stamping his name on nature.

Nature sighs and plans a winter of frosts. It prepares its arsenal of weedseeds. It is patient. And so is Horace. 'Nunc est bibendum,' says Horace, which translates loosely as 'Who's for the Pig and Chisel?'

Room

I write this in bed in the afternoon in the country in winter in a motel room that looks like the administrative office of Pukesville, Sadship and Grimm.

T.S. Eliot wrote of restless nights in one-night cheap hotels. Eliot didn't know the half of it. His hotels had sawdust floors and oyster shells. My motel has a carpet that can damage the retina.

The country in these parts is flat, empty and wet. The motel room is worse. It just doesn't bear thinking about. Yet I am thinking about it. I don't want to think about it. I don't want to write about it. But it empties the mind of all thoughts except razor blades. This is the motel where decor came to die. It makes me want to spit out all the butt-ends of my days and ways. And how shall I begin?

Vertebrae C1 to C6 are screaming. I have wedged the two Ethiopian charity-case pillows under the small of my back where they have burrowed irretrievably between the wall and the end of thing that the proprietor would no doubt call a mattress. The weight of my chest, head, trapezoids, deltoids, pecs, abs and other flab is applied through the back of my head against the sort of floral wallpaper that is made out of recycled Bulgarian ration-books and which the health departments of better countries banned in 1953. And that's the pretty wall. The other walls are concrete blocks painted regurgitation pastel.

The bed is covered with a ridged nylon bedspread the colour of something that needs to be drained. In an effort to shield my eyes from it I have littered the bedspread with the 7000 sections of the Sunday newspaper which focus on real estate and an activity called Living. Living seems to mean quilting clubs in the Manawatu, novels by women with armpits, the recipe for a Peruvian sardine dish with chives, and scrofular adolescents from Glasgow who are pleased to call themselves a 'band'. If that's Living I want nothing to do with it. And there isn't enough of it to cover the bedspread.

I am on the bed because I am not at the table. The table is worse than the bed. The table is in marble-finish formica, of course, on tubular chrome, of course, and it is littered with brochures for activities that would traumatise the dead. You can visit the new seed-drill display at the art and craft museum, tour the historic woolshed or trek with a spavinned pony. Against the table stand two chairs of chrome and plastic which attracted no bidders at the sort of auction attended by people with trackpants and limps.

The bathroom contains neither a bath nor room. The walls weep. The shower would scald the bristles off a pig and then freeze it for later. It will do nothing in between. And you couldn't fit a pig into it anyway. The thin nylon curtain stays cold under hot water and clings to wet flesh like a squid. It thinks it's a towel, except it doesn't dry you. Nor do the towels. The towels are sand-paper.

It is easy to enter the toilet by simply sucking in the stomach, flattening oneself against the weeping wall and shuffling sideways. I have just swung a cat in the toilet and killed it instantly. Had it been able to, it would have thanked me. The cat will never have to return to the kitchenette to see the plastic salt-cellar or the patterned plates or the unused potato masher in the drawer that sticks.

Tomorrow morning the cat will not have to face the continental breakfast that comes from no continent yet inhabited by mankind. That breakfast will be delivered to the door on a plastic tray by the proprietor and will comprise a bowl of four canned apricots, two slices of rectilinear suet bread, and individual portions of a polyunsaturated spread that tastes of desperation.

No doubt lots of motels are fine places. The last one I stayed in had milk in glass bottles, a heater that heated, tolerable furniture and a television that I eventually managed to turn on.

But this place sears the soul. And I haven't even mentioned the pictures on the walls. Nor am I going to. I haven't the words. You'll have to imagine them. And besides, I've decided to leave. I'm going home to soothe the soul with dogs and T.S. Eliot.

A woman on men

People who write about 'gender differences' make plenty of money and little sense. Latest to plough this profitable literary paddock is a Ms Jennifer Coates, a British academic who has just spent three months here denigrating men.

Ms Coates issued tape recorders to men who recorded their conversations and then, astonishingly, handed over the tapes. Ms Coates has analysed those tapes and reached conclusions as fresh as yesterday.

'Men… swear a lot, pay huge attention to detail and focus on impersonal topics,' discovers Ms Coates, and then with that piercing academic perception which has taken her to a professorship in sociolinguistics, 'I think the aim of all this swearing, detail and impersonal topics is to keep talk away from the personal.'

There's lots more of this generalising guff that I cannot bring myself to repeat, but in short, men get it wrong and women right. Men boast, bully and lie whereas women don't.

Obviously Ms Coates didn't hand out a tape recorder to the woman I sat next to at a dinner not so long ago who had all the charm of a front-end loader and who told me in such detail of the sexual, social and commercial triumphs of her sons and daughters, all of whom were individually capable of righting the world's wrongs, and whose merits reflected so spectacularly on their mother who 'didn't know where they got it from, I'm sure', that by the time dessert appeared I found I had tied my serviette into a noose. Nor did Ms Coates analyse the rhetoric of the Prime Minister and the Right Honourable Leader of the Opposition as they boast, taunt, cavil and fib their way around the country.

No, she reached the conclusions she sought, and delivered them in a learned academic paper entitled 'So I thought bollocks to that'. 'Men sometimes,' she says, 'do try to break though the bounds and talk about the real personal stuff', but if men think that what they are doing when they talk to each other 'is friendship, it is a very impoverished friendship'.

Yes, yes, dull men boast and swear and talk about the rugby they don't play, the punches they never threw and the sex they only imagined, and yes they are the sort of men who bore like drills and who listen to radio sport. For men have bragged since they first snared a mammoth and Ms Coates is telling us only what a hundred novelists and playwrights have observed.

'...the way to keep Peter amused was to get him to brag about his past iniquities,' writes Evelyn Waugh in 1941 of one of his characters in *Put Out More Flags*. Or let us nip back 350 more years to that bore Polonius who so wants to be seen as wise that he reveals himself a fool. Or a further 200 years to the braggart Miller in *The Canterbury Tales*, frantic to put one over on the Reeve.

But on the way let us look, too, at Shakespeare's Falstaff, a man whom Ms Coates would condemn, and rightly, as a lying, cheating, fornicating thief, braggart and drunk, a man whose taped conversations would make Ms Coates' eyes water. Yet this man Falstaff so relished life that the grave did gape 'thrice wider' for him than for other men. And this man Falstaff so enchanted both his audience and his creator that Shakespeare had to kill him off to allow Henry V to take centre stage.

And while we are there let us also look at the sensitivities of Hamlet, or the perspicacity of Feste or the wit of Benedick. And at the same time let us observe the malice of King Lear's daughters or the self-deluding mawkishness of the Countess Olivia. And let us conclude that there are and always have been dull men and bright men, good men and bad, braggarts and thinkers, fools and sages, just as there have been women of all these sorts.

And let us cease to examine men as if they were some species of animal with an ego like a set of antlers, driven to rut and fight and boast by instincts beyond their control, and let us banish the word 'gender' from the lexicon and Ms Coates and her kind from our shores and our minds, and let us see people as people.

Bronzino, the brat and the bird

A psychiatrist has just sent me a postcard from Florence. All postcards carry the same message: Having a wonderful time. Glad you're not here. Love from the hamster who's left the cage. PS. Please feel envy.

I do envy the psychiatrist but I am also grateful to her. Her postcard has introduced me to the fat brat.

The fat brat is 455 years old. In 1545 he was painted in all his fatness by a chap called Bronzino. At the time Bronzino was forty-two and the fat brat was about eighteen months.

The brat is so fat that his knuckles are dimples. In the cross-eyed manner of infants he is staring at the painter and gurgling with plump pleasure. At any moment he will dribble. The dribble will fall on a doublet of velvet. The cloth's as thick as a wad of money and the colour of raspberries and its seams are sewn with gold thread.

The brat's left hand dangles empty. The right clutches a goldfinch. The bird is clearly alive but the brat is far too self-satisfied to pay it attention. But Bronzino has paid the bird attention. With a skill detectable even on a postcard he has captured the tiny curve of its beak, the scarlet splash of its face, the black hood like a cowl and the slash of gold across its wings which lends the bird its name.

My grandfather had a goldfinch. I remember it on Saturday afternoons hopping in apparent boredom between the two perches in its cage while my grandfather smoked and watched horse racing on a black and white television in a darkened room and my grandmother sucked Imperial mints. I was as bored as the bird. Goldfinches sing like metallic water but I do not remember hearing this bird sing.

Bronzino got the goldfinch right. From the window as I write I can see goldfinches on a telephone wire. The birds perch briefly in ones and twos, allowing me a glimpse of their nervous brilliance. I see the scarlet face, the startling bands of gold. I glance from the postcard to the birds, a distance of 450 years. Nothing's changed. Then the goldfinches scatter. They fly in pulses, like little heartbeats. Sometimes on the Port Hills I see huge mobs of goldfinches pecking at the seed-tufts of thistles or clinging to the swaying stems of grasses. When I scare them they rise like a tiny storm and clamour.

And just as he captured the goldfinch Bronzino captured the child and all he stood for. You can sense from the painting that the infant mouth is stuffed with silver spoons. For though the child's Christian name was plain Giovanni, his surname was Medici.

The Medicis ruled Florence for 300 years. The first Medici made money from banking, turned his florins into power and then handed it down. Some of his descendants ruled as tyrants and made a lot more money. Others didn't and didn't. From the way little Giovanni is clutching the goldfinch I fancy he would have prospered.

Three Medicis became pope and one, Lorenzo the Magnificent, magnificently made his son a cardinal at the age of fourteen. That trinity of blood ties, money and power is as old as history. It goes on. You could see it in the stands in the Olympic opening ceremony. There sat poor Chelsea Clinton like a Medici child. There sat Bill Gates the Magnificent grinning like a strange one.

The Medicis were patrons of the arts. They sponsored not only Bronzino but also Leonardo and Michelangelo. They wanted themselves and their offspring and their glory recorded by the best talent they could buy. They bought, in short, immortality.

But just as the goldfinch goes on, and the dynasties of power go on, so, too, does irony. 500 years ago the Medicis built an office block from which to run their government more efficiently, and the building still stands. Its use, however, has changed. Today it is the Uffizi museum. When the psychiatrist visited Florence it was the first place that she went to, along with a million others. She went to pay homage, but not to the Medicis.

For when the tourists stare at the painting of the double-chinned child it is not Giovanni Medici that they see. What they see is what Bronzino saw, the Medicis as they were, smug with power and superfluous wealth. And, transcending every Medici who ever lived, they see the durability of art and the brilliance of a bird.

Indeed the Uffizi is like a postcard to the past. 'Dear Medicis,' it reads, 'Weather in the twenty-first century wonderful. Sorry you couldn't join us. But your hireling Bronzino is here and in very good form. He sends his regards. Love, Time.'

Standing for nothing

I know my godson's name but he does not know mine. Shortly after he was born I sent him a present but he didn't write back so that was the end of that. But I have just learned that if his parents should perish in a car crash I will become responsible for my godson's moral education. Poor little darling. I wish his parents long and happy lives and I suggest they buy a Volvo.

My relationship with my godson resembles my relationship with God. Once or twice in times of stress I've tried to ring God but he hasn't answered the phone. I have spoken only to his secretary, Miss Time, an ancient spinster, all bosom and tweed. Miss Time always tells me that God's in a meeting and asks if she could be of help. I unburden myself to her and she offers unchanging advice. 'Wait,' she says, 'be patient. This too will pass.' She's right, of course, but it always takes a while for things to get better and by then I can't be bothered to write and thank her. In which respect, I suppose, I'm as ungrateful as my godson. But actually I prefer Miss Time to God. God's too definite for me. He's got strong opinions.

I once knew a school chaplain who wore short shorts and read short prayers. Children, he said, paid little attention to long prayers. I could have told him that they paid scant attention to any prayers, but I didn't because, well, I just didn't. Anyway, his favourite prayer ran thus: 'O Lord, let me stand for something lest I fall for anything. Amen.'

This prayer impressed me by its brevity, its memorability, its neat antithetical construction and its profound and unmatchable stupidity. It suggests that any opinion is better than no opinion. It suggests that having no opinion is dangerous. The truth of the world is precisely the opposite. Opinions are bad things.

By opinions I do not mean ideas, and I do not mean thought. An opinion is rarely born of thought. Instead it arrives fully formed in a head. Opinions are, as I have written elsewhere, almost always emotion in fancy dress. They can be inherited, or they can spring from fears or desires, but they are never right.

Yet look how ferociously, how indefatigably, people cling to their opinions in the face of a flood of evidence that those opinions are at best questionable, and more likely mere dump fodder.

Look at the intransigent folly of so much politics. Look at the nonsense that passes for political debate. Listen to the roaring when a political opponent slips. Hear the deep delighted belly laughs when Marian Hobbs gets confused. That isn't debate. That's merely a primal contest for power in which one side has caught a glimpse of an unprotected jugular. Yet if you want to take part in this contest you are required to join a team and in order to join a team you have to have a packaged set of opinions.

Where do those opinions come from? Are they arrived at by rational analysis? If so, and if reason is reason, how come they differ? But opinions are not reasonable.

We are emotional creatures in an irrational world. Anyone who holds opinions is wrong and dangerous. The European colonists of the nineteenth century were wrong and dangerous. Karl Marx was wrong and dangerous. George Speight is wrong and dangerous.

The only comfortable seat for a thinking human being is a fence. How is it, when we know so much about human nature from Shakespeare's plays, know more indeed than we could hope to garner from any other source, that we know so little about Shakespeare's opinions? The answer is that he doubted. He was a fence-sitter, an observer, a puppeteer who jigged his little figures about on stage and made them hold every opinion which was popular in the sixteenth century – and which, oddly enough, are the same opinions as are popular in the twenty-first – and he set his opinionated characters to play out their dramas of conflict and resolution, of crowns and thorns, of love and loss, of birth and death while he himself sat in among them smiling gently, tolerantly on their fierce little blindnesses. Shakespeare knew the primacy of emotion and the supreme virtue of doubt.

So if my buddy God should move in that mysterious way of

his and drop a thunderbolt or a tree on the Volvo that belongs to my old friends Philip and Olivia and thereby squash them dead, then I shall indeed accept the duty of a godfather. And when I greet my grief-stricken godson at the airport, I shall straightway seize him by the ankles and shake him until all opinions tumble out of him. And I shall then endeavour to fill the gap with doubt.

And, as has always been the way of the world, and as will always be the way of the world, the boy won't listen to a word I say. Just like everybody else, he will have to nose his own way through Miss Time's assault course, sniffing an idea here, a theory there, moving on, and nudging, one hopes, ever closer to the throne of doubt. Meanwhile I shall be on my knees in the cathedral, praying 'O Lord, let him stand for nothing lest he should believe it'. Not, of course, that I shall expect my prayer to be answered.

And that's my opinion.